CONTENTS

INTRODUCTION

What Is A Kamado Grill?

If 'kamado' sounds like a kind of martial arts, that's probably because kamado grills have their origins in Japan.

The word 'kamado' means "stove" in Japanese and is used to refer to a "place for the cauldron."

A portable version caught the attention of hungry U.S. soldiers stationed in Japan after the Second World War and soon made it's way Stateside. Without delving deep into the history, in time, the Kamado evolved into the egg-shaped grills we know today.

How do Kamado Grills Work?

Kamados are made from a variety of materials, including stainless steel and cast aluminum. The best kamados, however, are made of ceramics.

This material makes them very heavy and a bit fragile, but it also retains and radiates heat with amazing efficiency – and that's what makes a kamado so great.

A charcoal fire built in the firebox – towards the base of the Kamado – draws air in from a vent near the bottom to provide a controlled amount of oxygen to the fire.

Heat and smoke are then drawn up through the cooking chamber towards the vent at the top, passing over and around the food on the cooking grates as it goes.

The ceramic material absorbs and radiates heat for incredibly even, all-over cooking. Food on the grates is slowly or quickly cooked, depending on the style of cooking chosen.

The Pros of Owning the Char-Griller Kamado Grills

1. When treated properly, ceramic kamados will last a very, very long time. So think hard about the model you purchase, as it might even be passed on to your kids. Make it a good one!

2. The top-notch insulation of these units means that they are easy to start even in inclement weather. If you live in a cold climate and want to smoke through the winter, Kamados are a great option as they provide excellent heat retention and even cooking temperature.

3. Kamado grills are very efficient. You will find that you will chew through a relatively small amount of charcoal for the length of time you can smoke.

4. Flare ups are rare in ceramic cookers as the meat sits further away from the coals.

5. Your meat will remain moist and juicy when using a ceramic cooker. This is because less moisture is able to evaporate out of the meat due to decreased airflow.

6. Firing up a kamado requires a different technique than other charcoal grills. Once you have mastered this technique, however, they are very easy to get going.

7. You are able to cook at a wide variety of temperatures with these units. From cold smoking jerky to cooking a pizza, once you have mastered the temperature control on these, you are able to do a lot.

Tricks on Using Your Char-Griller Kamado Grill

1. Play Around With Airborne Heat

When you begin to cook with your Kamado grill, adjust the damper at the top and bottom. The more air that flows into your Kamado grill, the hotter the temperature is going to get. The less air you circulate, the cooler the temperature.

Why is this important? Basically, you would never want to sear a chicken on the outside only to discover it was pink and raw in the middle! Therefore, to regulate your temperature on the grill, you should always control the air going in and coming out.

Again, this is a lot of art mixed with science. Practice definitely makes perfect. Be sure to use a thermometer to make sure all your meat hits the sweet spot temperature-wise before serving.

2. Have Multiple Heating Zones

Want another quickie way to control how hot your Kamado grill gets? Just pile the charcoal differently below different "zones" on your grill. For example, visually divide your charcoal grill in half. Place a regular amount of charcoal on one side, and then double that amount on the other side.

The closer your food is to the heat source, the hotter and faster it will cook. Therefore, if you have some Kamado recipes that call for fast cooking at hot temperatures, you can cook them simultaneously with a recipe that calls for slower cooking with less heat. Basically, you can create a dual burner. You can even set it up so your Kamado grill has three zones. Again, experiment to see what works best.

3. Raise or Lower Your Grill Grate

Love the idea of having a grill grate that can be different heights? Put it to use every time you do a little Kamado grill cooking. That way, you can be sure you keep certain items away from the flames, or bring others closer when you want a little more char or intense heat.

Tips on How Often to Clean Your Char-Griller Kamado Grill

A Big Green Egg is an investment. In order to get the most for your money, it is important to take care of your grill so that it will last for years to come. A good cleaning will allow you to remove most of the gunk that has been accumulated over many instances of cooking and BBQ smoking. While some Eggheads will argue you never have to clean your grill, most agree that removing excess oil and grease will improve the quality of your cooking.

There are a few ways to clean your grill, from burning off stuck-on grime after using your grill to a full wipe-down and ash clearing. The type of cleaning you do will depend on how often you do it.

Important note: since the Big Green Egg is ceramic, never use alcohol or other cleaning chemicals. This will cause the chemicals to seep into the surface and will impart a bad taste to your food. Similarly, do not use water to clean the Egg. Water can be absorbed into the Egg and may crack the surface with repeated heating and cooling.

1. Things to do every time you cook

After you cook, it is a good idea to close your Egg and let it continue to burn for a while, then scrape the steel grill with a grid tool and/or steel mesh brush. This helps to remove any excess food particles that are stuck on. If you do this every time, you will not have to worry about an overload of junk inside your Egg. You can also use a scrubber to clean the baking stone or heat plate. Scrape off the Conveggtor if you used that as well. Use an ash tool to stir the ash from the coals.

2. Things to do every so often (3-5 cooks)

While the Big Green Egg doesn't create a lot of ash, it's smart to clean it out every few cooks to make it easier to bring your grill up to temperature and keep it that way. All you have to do is use an ash tool to brush through the remaining coals once they have cooled. You can reuse these. The rest of the ash that falls through the grate can be removed with an ash tool and discarded. You can also wipe down the exterior with a cloth to get rid of any dust or ash and wipe the vent on top with some light cooking oil.

3. Deep cleaning

While opinions vary, it's not a bad idea to give your Egg a good deep cleaning a few times a year. This means removing all the inner parts and removing the stuck-on food and liquids, ash and other bits of debris in your grill. Clean the interior with a plastic bristled-brush or use a ball of aluminum to remove any leftover gunk. You can use a shop-vac to get all the ash out of the bottom of your egg. To perform a self-clean, much like an oven, replace all the parts and add charcoal. Then bring your grill up to around 600 degrees and let it burn for about an hour. Make sure to clean out the vent holes afterward.

FISH AND SEAFOOD

Smoked King Salmon

Servings: 8

Cooking Time: 75 Minutes

Ingredients:

- 2lb (1kg) skinless King salmon fillets
- for the brine
- 1/2 cup kosher salt
- 1/2 cup packed light brown sugar
- 3 tbsp pickling spice
- 6 cups hot water
- for the pesto
- 5 tbsp extra virgin olive oil, divided
- 1/4 cup walnut halves
- 2 cups baby arugula, loosely packed
- 1 cup fresh basil leaves, loosely packed
- 3 tbsp freshly grated Parmigiano-Reggiano
- 1 garlic clove
- kosher salt and freshly ground black pepper
- to smoke
- alder or cedar wood chunks

Directions:

1. To make the brine, in a medium bowl, whisk together salt, brown sugar, pickling spice, and water until salt and sugar have dissolved. Add ice cubes until the liquid is no longer hot. Place salmon in a resealable plastic bag, add the brine to cover, and refrigerate for 30 minutes. (Any extra brine can be refrigerated and saved for a later use.)

2. Remove salmon from the brine, pat dry with paper towels, and refrigerate until the surface begins to look dry and feel slightly tacky, about 30 to 60 minutes more.

3. Preheat the grill to 225°F (107°C) using indirect heat. Once hot, add the wood chunks and install a cast iron grate and a cast iron skillet. Place 1 tbsp oil and walnuts in the skillet, close the lid, and cook until they just begin to toast, about 10 to 15 minutes. Remove the walnuts from the grill and let cool.

4. To make the pesto, in a food processor, combine walnuts, arugula, basil, Parmigiano-Reggiano, and garlic. Process until the mixture is finely chopped. With the processor running, slowly add 4 tbsp oil until well combined. Thin the pesto with 1 tbsp water (if desired). Transfer to a bowl and season with salt and pepper to taste.

5. Place salmon on the grate, close the lid, and cook until the fish reaches an internal temperature of 135°F (57°C) and just begins to flake, about 45 to 60 minutes. Remove salmon from the grill, and serve immediately with the pesto.

Grilled Tuna Burger

Servings:4

Cooking Time: 10 Minutes

Ingredients:

- 2 (7 ounce) pounches albacore tuna, or 2 (6 ounce) cans albacore tuna in water
- 1 cup panko (Japanese breadcrumbs)
- ¼ cup chopped onion
- ¼ cup chopped celery
- Salt and pepper to taste
- ¼ teaspoon Old Bay seasoning
- 1 (14.5 ounce) can can Red Gold Petite Diced Tomatoes W/Lime Juice & Cilantro, drained
- 2 eggs, beaten
- 4 hamburger buns
- 4 tablespoons dill dip

Directions:

1. Preheat the grill to 350°F using direct heat with a cast iron grate installed.
2. In a large bowl combine tuna, bread crumbs, onion, celery, salt, black pepper, Old Bay seasoning, Red Gold Tomatoes and eggs; mix well. Shape into 4 patties, ¾ inch thick. Refrigerate for 30 minutes before cooking.
3. Spray grates with cooking spray. Place patties on kamado grill and cook 8 to 10 minutes until deep golden brown, turning once.
4. Place a tablespoon of dill dip on the bottom of the bun. Top with tuna patty and top half of bun.
5. Option: Add a leaf of lettuce and a slice of red onion.
6. Option:The tuna burgers can be made ahead of time and stored in the refrigerator overnight.

Tuna Kabobs

Servings:2

Cooking Time: 10 Minutes

Ingredients:

- 2 tuna steaks, cut into 2-inch pieces
- 1 large red bell pepper, cut into 2-inch pieces
- 1 sweet onion, cut into 2-inch pieces
- 1 pineapple, cut into 2-inch pieces
- 1 cup Sweet Kentucky Bourbon Grilling Glaze
- Salt and pepper to taste

Directions:

1. Preheat the grill to 350°F using direct heat with a cast iron grate installed.
2. Thread the tuna, red bell peppers, onion and pineapple onto the skewers, leaving a small space between each item. Salt and pepper to taste.
3. Grill for 5 minutes then brush on the Sweet Kentucky Bourbon Grilling Glaze on both sides. Grill for another 5 minutes; glaze once more and remove from the kamado grill. Let rest for 10 minutes. Enjoy!

Salt Baked Snapper

Servings:6

Cooking Time: 20 Minutes

Ingredients:

- 4 pounds Kosher salt
- 3 egg whites
- 1 whole snapper (4-5 pounds cleaned)
- ¼ cup extra-virgin olive oil
- Lemon wedges

Directions:

1. Preheat the grill to 550°F using direct heat with a cast iron grate installed.

2. Mix salt and egg whites in a big bowl and mix until light and fluffy. Spread ¼ of the salt mixture on a thick pan covered with aluminum foil. Place cleaned fish onto the salt on the pan and cover with the rest of the salt mixture.

3. Place the dish in the grill and cook until internal temperature reaches 130°F. When done, let rest 10 minutes. Place fish on a platter and crack the salt crust with a hammer to reveal the tender fish.

4. Serve with grilled lemon wedges, fennel and herb salad drizzled with olive oil.

Zesty Cedar Planked Cod

Servings:4

Cooking Time: 15 Minutes

Ingredients:

- 2 5-8 oz cod loin portions
- 1 orange, zested
- 1 lemon, zested
- 1 lime, zested
- 1 tbsp peppercorn medley, ground
- Kosher salt
- Olive oil
- Cedar Grilling Planks

Directions:

1. Preheat the grill to 400°F using direct heat with a cast iron grate installed. Soak the plank in hot water for at least 15 minutes.

2. Rub the cod with olive oil and sprinkle with salt and pepper. Combine the 3 citrus zests and place equal amounts on each piece of cod.

3. Set the cod on the cedar planks and place in the kamado grill. Cook for 10-15 minutes or until the cod reaches an internal temperature of 125°F.

4. Remove from the kamado grill and serve immediately. Enjoy!

Seafood & Smoked Gouda Pasta

Servings: 12

Cooking Time: 40 Minutes

Ingredients:

- 1 red bell pepper, halved
- 4 asparagus stalks
- 8 tbsp olive oil
- 8 garlic cloves, minced
- 2lb (1kg) raw seafood, such as shrimp, scallops, or white fish, thawed if frozen
- kosher salt and freshly ground black pepper
- 16oz (450g) dried vermicelli
- crushed red pepper flakes, to garnish
- chopped fresh flat-leaf parsley, to garnish
- for the sauce
- 2 cups heavy cream
- 1/2 cup unsalted butter, softened
- 1/2 cup grated smoked gouda
- freshly ground black pepper

Directions:

1. Preheat the grill to 350°F (177°C) using direct heat with a cast iron grate installed and a dutch oven on the grate. Place pepper and asparagus on the grate (not in the dutch oven), close the grill lid, and grill until beginning to soften and char, about 7 to 10 minutes. Remove from the grill, chop, and set aside.

2. To the hot dutch oven, add olive oil and garlic. Cook until fragrant, about 30 seconds. Add seafood, season well with salt and pepper, and close the grill lid. Cook until seafood has begun to look opaque and take on color, about 5 minutes, stirring once. Transfer the cooked seafood to a cutting board and return the dutch oven to the grill. Cut seafood into bite-sized pieces. Set aside.

3. To make the sauce, add cream and butter to the hot dutch oven, and whisk gently until butter has melted. Sprinkle in smoked gouda, and stir to incorporate. Season with freshly ground black pepper to taste. Close the grill lid and reduce the cream sauce until just thickened, about 10 minutes, stirring occasionally.

4. On the stovetop, cook vermicelli according to package directions until cooked but still firm to the bite. Drain briefly in a colander.

5. Add seafood, pasta, and vegetables to the dutch oven. Gently toss to coat with the sauce. Garnish with crushed red pepper flakes and parsley. Serve immediately.

Grilled Red Snapper

Servings: 6
Cooking Time: 20 Minutes

Ingredients:

- 2 whole red snapper, about 4lb (1.8kg) in total
- kosher salt and freshly ground black pepper
- 3 lemons, thinly sliced, plus more lemon wedges to serve
- 4 garlic cloves, peeled
- 2-in (5-cm) piece fresh ginger, peeled and thinly sliced
- a few sprigs of fresh oregano
- a few sprigs of fresh flat-leaf parsley, plus leaves to garnish
- 2 tbsp extra virgin olive oil
- for the sauce
- 1/2 cup extra virgin olive oil, plus more for grilling
- 2 medium garlic cloves
- 2 red onions, halved
- 4 Roma tomatoes, roughly chopped
- 2 tsp minced fresh oregano

Directions:

1. Preheat the grill to 400°F (204°C) using direct heat with a cast iron grate installed. Brush onion halves with oil, place on the grate, close the lid, and grill until beginning to soften and char, about 4 to 6 minutes. Remove from the grill, let cool slightly, and roughly chop.

2. To make the sauce, in a food processor, combine oil, garlic, and half the onions, and pulse until they form a coarse paste. Add tomatoes and oregano, and pulse briefly until the sauce has a chunky, salsa-like consistency. Transfer to a bowl and stir in reserved onion. Season with black pepper to taste and set aside.

3. Remove fish from the fridge and let come to room temperature. Thoroughly pat dry with paper towels, then season inside and out with salt and pepper to taste. Stuff with lemon slices, garlic, ginger slices, and oregano and parsley sprigs. Rub the exterior with oil.

4. Place fish on the grate, close the lid, and grill until the bottom sides brown, about 5 minutes. Using a spatula, carefully attempt to lift the fish from below. If they resist, allow them to cook for 1 minute more and try again. When fish lift easily from the grill, flip and continue to grill until fish begin to flake and an instant-read thermometer inserted in the thickest part reads 135°F (57°C), about 7 to 10 minutes.

5. Transfer to a serving platter and let rest for 5 minutes. Spoon the tomato sauce over top, and garnish with freshly chopped parsley. Serve with lemon wedges.

Grilled Oysters

Servings:2

Cooking Time: 5 Minutes

Ingredients:

- A dozen fresh oysters (the fresher, closer-to-home you can get the better!)
- 6 Tbsp – a little more than half a package – slow-cultured, Roasted Garlic Basil & Parsley Banner Butter
- 1 lemon, cut into slices or wedges
- 3 Tbsp fresh chives, roughly chopped

Directions:

1. Preheat the grill to 425°F using direct heat with a cast iron grate installed.
2. Take your Roasted Garlic Basil & Parsley Banner Butter out of the fridge and set aside in a small bowl.
3. Carefully shuck the oysters with a small knife (an oyster knife with a rounded tip and a work glove on the hand grasping the oyster is a good choice for novice shuckers). Remove the top, flat shell and discard. Place the rounded (bowl side of the shell) side with the oyster on a Perforated Cooking Grid.
4. Place the Perforated Grid in the kamado grill and then add a half tablespoon of softened Roasted Garlic butter to each oyster.
5. Close the lid and kamado grill for 4 or 5 minutes until the oysters are bubbling (not rubbery). The butter should be completely melted and beginning to caramelize on the shell when done.
6. Remove from the kamado grill and move the oysters to a serving plate with the lemons. Squeeze a few wedges/slices onto the oysters and then scatter the chives across the plate.

Cedar-plank Salmon

Servings: 4
Cooking Time: 15 Minutes

Ingredients:

- 11/2lb (680g) skinless salmon, cut from the thickest part of the fish
- for the brine
- 2⁄3 cup kosher salt
- 2⁄3 cup packed light brown sugar
- 4 tbsp pickling spice
- 8 cups hot water
- for the sauce
- 2 limes
- 2 garlic cloves, minced
- 1 tbsp extra virgin olive oil
- 1 tbsp honey
- 1 tbsp soy sauce
- 1 tsp chopped fresh mint leaves, plus more to garnish
- 1-in (2.5-cm) piece ginger, peeled and grated
- kosher salt and freshly ground black pepper

Directions:

1. Place a 4 x 9in (10 x 23cm) cedar wood plank in a baking dish, cover with cold water, and place heavy cans or stones on the plank to keep it submerged. Soak for 1 to 2 hours.

2. To make the brine, in a large bowl, whisk together salt, brown sugar, pickling spice, and water until salt and sugar have dissolved. Add ice cubes a few at a time until the liquid is no longer hot. Place the salmon in a large resealable plastic bag and add brine to fully cover. (Any extra brine can be refrigerated and saved for a later use.) Refrigerate for 1 hour.

3. To make the sauce, grate the zest from 1 lime into a small bowl. Squeeze the juice of both limes and add to the bowl, then whisk in garlic, oil, honey, soy sauce, mint, and ginger. Taste and season with salt and pepper.

4. Preheat the grill to 400°F (204°C) using direct heat with a standard grate installed. Remove the cedar plank from the water and pat dry with paper towels. Place the plank on the grate until it starts to crackle and some coloring and charring appear, about 3 minutes, then turn the plank over.

5. Remove salmon from the brine and place it on the hot side of the plank. Generously brush salmon with lime sauce, close the lid, and grill until the fish is just cooked through and slightly flaky but still moist, about 12 to 15 minutes.

6. Remove salmon from the grill, lightly brush with some of the remaining sauce, and garnish with mint leaves. Serve immediately.

Cedar-planked Salmon With Sweet Chili Sauce

Servings:4

Cooking Time: 27 Minutes

Ingredients:

- 2 Salmon filets cut to fit a Cedar Plank
- Sweet & Smoky Seasoning
- Thai sweet chile sauce

Directions:

1. Preheat the grill to 350°F using direct heat with a cast iron grate installed.
2. Place the cedar planks in a pan, cover with water and soak for about 2 hours.
3. Season the salmon with Sweet & Smoky Seasoning. Warm the Thai Chili Sauce in the sauce pot.
4. Place the plank on cooking grid, close the dome and heat for about 2 minutes. Using tongs, flip the plank, and then place a salmon on heated side of plank. Coat the salmon with the warm sauce. Close the dome and cook for 20-25 minutes.
5. Remove from the plank from the kamado grill and serve.

Grilled Shrimp

Servings:4

Cooking Time: 18 Minutes

Ingredients:

- 1 lb shrimp, 16/20 size, peeled and deveined
- ¼ cup olive oil
- ¼ cup lemon juice
- 3 tbsp fresh chopped parsley
- Coarse salt and freshly cracked pepper
- 1 cup dry white wine
- 1 cup shallots minced
- ½ cup unsalted butter, cut into ½ inch cubes, chilled
- 1 tbsp Citrus & Dill Sauce Seasoning
- 1 tbsp fresh lemon juice

Directions:

1. Preheat the grill to 450°F using direct heat with a cast iron grate installed.
2. In a large, non-reactive bowl, stir together the olive oil, lemon juice, parsley, salt and black pepper. Add shrimp and toss to coat. Marinate in the refrigerator for 30 minutes.
3. For the sauce: In a small saucepan, heat the wine and shallots over medium-high heat until reduced to 2 tablespoons, about 12-15 minutes. Turn off the heat and gradually add each cube of butter into the reduction, whisking after each
4. addition. Add the Citrus & Dill Seasoning, and season with salt as desired. Whisk in the lemon juice and set sauce aside.
5. Place the shrimp on a lightly oiled Perforated Cooking Grid and cook for 2 to 3 minutes per side, or until opaque. Serve the shrimp drizzled with the sauce over quinoa or rice.

Florida Lobster Roll

Servings:6

Cooking Time: 28 Minutes

Ingredients:

- 4 tablespoons butter, divided
- Garlic powder
- 3 Florida lobster tails, about 7 ounces each
- ½ cup mayonnaise
- Zest from ½ of a Florida orange
- 1/3 cup finely chopped celery
- Pinch dried tarragon
- 6 hot dog buns, top split if available
- Slices of Florida avocado
- Spinach leaves

Directions:

1. Preheat the grill to 350°F using direct heat with a cast iron grate installed.
2. Split the top of the lobster shells and pull the meat out to rest on top. Cut a few slits in the meat so the lobster will cook evenly (you can have your fish monger do this for you). Place the tails on a perforated cooking grid and season lightly with salt and pepper.
3. Melt two tablespoons of butter and mix in a pinch of garlic powder. Brush the tails liberally with the butter. Place in the kamado grill and cook until the tails are firm to the touch, about 25 minutes; remove and let cool.
4. Remove the platesetter to cook direct at 350°F/177°C. Melt the remaining butter and mix in a pinch of garlic powder. Brush the sides of the rolls and grill them for 2 to 3 minutes on each side until golden brown. Remove the lobster meat from the shells and cut into large dice. Add to the dressing and mix well. Line each bun with a few spinach leaves. Lay a few slices of avocado in the bun and top each with an equal portion of the lobster mix.
5. Mix ingredients together in a large bowl.

Shrimp & Cheddar Tostada

Servings:6

Cooking Time: 10 Minutes

Ingredients:

- ¼ cup fat free cream cheese, softened
- ¼ cup reduced-fat mayonnaise
- 2 tablespoons skim milk
- ¼ cup finely chopped fresh cilantro
- 2 tablespoons fresh lime juice, divided
- 30 medium-size shrimp, peeled and deveined (about 1 pound)
- 2 tablespoons barbecue rub or seasoning
- ½ teaspoon salt
- Cooking spray
- 6 (6-inch) corn tortillas
- 4 ounces Cabot Jalapeno Light Cheddar or Cabot Sharp Light Cheddar, grated (about 1 cup)
- 6 tablespoons finely chopped fresh tomato

Directions:

1. In small bowl, combine cream cheese, mayonnaise and milk; whisk until smooth. Stir in cilantro and 1 tablespoon of lime juice. Cover and refrigerate until serving time.

2. When ready to serve, thread 5 shrimp onto flexible skewers. In small bowl, combine barbecue rub and salt. Brush shrimp with remaining 1 tablespoon lime juice and dredge in rub mixture. Place kabobs in shallow dish; cover and refrigerate for 15 minutes.

3. Preheat the grill to 350°F using direct heat with a cast iron grate installed.

4. Place kabobs on kamado grill grid coated with cooking spray and cook for 3 minutes on each side, or until done. Set aside.

5. Place tortillas directly on kamado grill and cook for 4 minutes. Top each tortilla with some of cheese and bake until cheese is melted, about 3 minutes longer.

6. Place 1 tortilla on each of 6 individual serving plates. Top each with 5 grilled shrimp and 2 tablespoons cilantro mayonnaise. Sprinkle with tomato and serve.

Bobby Flay's Grilled Lobster Sandwiches

Servings:6

Cooking Time: 28 Minutes

Ingredients:

- 4 (2-pound) live lobsters
- 8 ears of corn
- Kosher salt and freshly ground black pepper
- Canola oil
- 1 serrano chile
- 3 ripe Hass avocados, peeled, pitted, and diced
- 1/4 cup creme fraiche
- 1/2 small red onion, finely diced
- 1/4 cup chopped fresh cilantro leaves
- Juice of 2 limes
- Few dashes of Tabasco sauce
- 6 soft sesame seed buns, split
- Fresh flat-leaf parsley, for garnish

Directions:

1. Bring a large pot of salted water to a boil. Working in batches, add the lobsters and boil for 10 to 12 minutes; they will be about three-quarters done. Drain well and let cool. The lobsters can be parboiled a few hours in advance, covered, and kept refrigerated. Bring to room temperature before grilling.

2. Heat your grill to high for direct grilling.

3. Pull the outer husks down each ear of corn to the base. Strip away the silk from each ear of corn. Fold the husks back into place and tie the ends together with kitchen string. Place the ears of corn in a large bowl of cold water with 1 tablespoon salt for 10 minutes.

4. Remove the corn from the water and shake off the excess. Put the corn on the grill, close the cover, and grill, turning every 5 minutes, for 15 minutes, or until the kernels are almost tender when pierced with a paring knife.

5. Peel back the husks and remove. Brush the corn with oil and season with salt and pepper. Grill the ears until the kernels are lightly golden brown on all sides, about 5 minutes. Use a sharp knife to remove the kernels from the ears.

6. Brush the serrano with oil and grill, turning as needed, until charred all over, 6 to 8 minutes. Remove to a bowl, cover, and let sit for 10 minutes. Peel, seed, and roughly chop.

7. Put the avocados and crème fraîche in a medium bowl and mash slightly with a fork. Add the corn kernels, chile, diced red onion, cilantro, lime juice, Tabasco, and 2 tablespoons of oil. Season with salt and pepper and gently stir to combine.

8. Split each lobster down the underside with a heavy knife, taking care not to cut through the back shell, so that the lobster is still in one piece but the inside flesh is halved and exposed. Brush the cut sides of the lobsters with oil and season with salt and pepper. Grill the lobsters, cut side down, until lightly charred and heated through, 5 to 7 minutes.

9. Toast the buns, split side down, on the grill until lightly golden brown, about 20 seconds.

10. Remove the lobster meat from the shells and coarsely chop. Fill each bun with lobster, charred corn and avocado, and some parsley leaves.

Southwest Baked Oysters

Servings:2
Cooking Time: 15 Minutes

Ingredients:
- Clean oyster shells
- Olive oil
- Oysters
- Finely chopped jalapeno chiles
- Shredded cheddar cheese or grated parmesan cheese
- Bacon bits or soy bacon bits
- Italian-style seasoned bread crumbs

Directions:
1. Preheat the grill to 375°F using direct heat with a cast iron grate installed.
2. Arrange they oyster shells in a Perforated Cooking Grid. Spray with olive oil. Place 1 large or 2 small oysters in each shell. Top each with 2 or 3 tiny pieces of jalapeno. Sprinkle with cheese and bacon bits. Top with bread crumbs.
3. Place pan on the cooking grid and bake at 375° for 10 to 15 minutes or until bubbly; do not overcook.

Blackened Grouper

Servings:2
Cooking Time: 10 Minutes

Ingredients:
- Grouper (thick is best)
- Chef Paul Prudhomme's blackening seasoning
- Butter

Directions:
1. Preheat the grill to 500°F using direct heat with a cast iron grate installed.
2. Season grouper with seasoning.
3. Add butter to the griddle, followed by the grouper.
4. Cook for three minutes, flip grouper and cook for another three minutes.
5. Remove grouper from kamado grill and place on plate on top of cheese grits.

Crab Cakes

Servings:4

Cooking Time: 20 Minutes

Ingredients:

- 1 pound lump crabmeat, canned
- 2 large eggs, beaten
- 2 jalapenos, seeded and minced
- 1⁄2 cup Panko bread crumbs
- 1⁄2 cup mayonnaise
- 1 tablespoon chopped fresh parsley
- 2 teaspoons Dizzy Gourmet Viva Caliente Seasoning
- 1⁄2 cup Vidalia Onion Sriracha Sauce, or sweet barbecue sauce
- 1⁄2 cup ranch dressing

Directions:

1. Preheat the grill to 375°F using direct heat with a cast iron grate installed.
2. In a medium bowl, combine the eggs, jalapenos, panko, mayo, parsley and BGE seasoning. Mix well until blended.
3. Add the crab meat and fold together until well blended.
4. Form the crab mixture into 4 equal size balls. Smash them into thick patties.
5. Bake until golden brown, approximately 18-20 minutes.
6. Combine the barbecue sauce and the ranch dressing in a small bowl. Mix well. Serve the crab cakes with the barbecue ranch as a dipping sauce.

Clam Bake

Servings: 6
Cooking Time: 30 Minutes

Ingredients:

- 2 lbs mussels, scrubbed and debearded
- 1 1/2 lbs kielbasa sausage, sliced into 1 inch chunks
- 1 1/2 lbs small potatoes (we like red potatoes)
- 2 large onions, roughly chopped
- 2 dozen littleneck clams, scrubbed
- 2 dozen steamer clams, scrubbed
- 2 cups dry white wine
- 2 Tablespoons olive oil
- 1 Tablespoon salt
- 1/2 Tablespoon black pepper

Directions:

1. Preheat the grill to 350°F using direct heat with a cast iron grate installed with the dutch oven on the grid.
2. Add olive oil and onion to the pot and cook until soft, about 5 minutes.
3. Add ingredients in layers in the following order: Kielbasa, Potatoes, Clams, Mussels.
4. Pour in the white wine and cover.
5. Lower the dome for 15-20 minutes or until the potatoes are cooked through and the shellfish have opened up.
6. Ladle out the sausage, potatoes, and seafood and strain the broth, taking care not to get any sand from the clams.
7. Serve on sheets of parchment paper with broth in small bowls for dipping and sipping.
8. If you have never tried parsnips before, they look like a white carrot and taste like a cross between a carrot and horseradish. When they are braised they become sweet, a perfect alternative to plain carrots.

Grilled Asian Mahi-mahi

Servings:4
Cooking Time: 24 Minutes

Ingredients:

- 4 (1 inch thick) Mahi-Mahi filets
- 1 tablespoon Better Than Bouillon Fish Base
- 1/2 cup soy sauce
- 1 1/2 Tablespoon sesame oil
- 1 teaspoon honey
- 1/2 teaspoon garlic powder
- 2 teaspoons sesame seeds

Directions:

1. Preheat the grill to 400°F using direct heat with a cast iron grate installed.
2. Mix the fish base, soy sauce, sesame oil, honey and garlic powder in a medium-sized shallow bowl. Add the Mahi-Mahi to the bowl and marinate for 20 minutes.
3. Place the Mahi-Mahi directly onto the kamado grill and grill for 3-4 minutes per side.
4. Remove the fish from the grill, sprinkle with the sesame seeds and serve immediately.

Swordfish Steaks With Peach Salsa

Servings: 4

Cooking Time: 15 Minutes

Ingredients:

- 4 swordfish steaks (about 1 inch thick, or 6 ounces)
- 1 Tablespoon olive oil
- Salt & Pepper
- 1/4 cup finely diced red pell pepper
- 1 Tablespoon olive oil
- 1/4 tsp cumin
- 2 peaches, slightly underripe, diced
- 1 jalapeño, seeded and finely chopped
- The juice and zest of 1 lime

Directions:

1. Combine ingredients for the salsa and set aside.
2. Brush both sides of the swordfish steaks with olive oil and season with salt and pepper.
3. Grilling:
4. Preheat the grill to 400°F using direct heat with a cast iron grate installed.
5. Place the steaks directly on the grid and close the dome for 6 minutes.
6. Gently flip the fish and close the dome for another 6-8 minutes or until the fish is firm.
7. Remove from the grid and serve topped with peach salsa.

Grilled Shrimp And Taylor Farms Tangerine Crunch Wraps

Servings:2

Cooking Time: 6 Minutes

Ingredients:

- 1 lb. large shrimp, peeled and deveined
- Savory Pecan Seasoning
- 4-6 sundried tomato or spinach wraps
- 1 Taylor Farms Tangerine Crunch Chopped Kit
- bamboo skewers, soaked
- Feta cheese, optional

Directions:

1. Preheat the grill to 400°F using direct heat with a cast iron grate installed.
2. Season the shrimp on both sides with the Savory Pecan Seasoning. Skewer the shrimp with the soaked skewers.
3. Place the shrimp on the kamado grill and cook for 3 minutes per side or until the shrimp are pink and firm. Remove from the grill, cool and remove from the skewers.
4. Heat a plancha on the grill, griddle-side up.
5. Mix together the Taylor Farms Tangerine Crunch Chopped Kit. Fill the wrap with the salad, top with shrimp and feta cheese. Roll the wrap to enclose the salad. Heat the wrap on the plancha until you have your desired grill marks. Remove from the kamado grill and serve.

Morro Bay Bbq Cowboy Oysters

Servings:6

Cooking Time: 10 Minutes

Ingredients:

- 6 Morro Bay Jumbo Oysters, washed well
- ¼ lb butter
- 1 large shallot
- A "good splash" of bourbon
- 2 teaspoons your favorite BBQ spice
- Lemon
- ½ bunch chives, sliced

Directions:

1. Preheat the grill to 400°F using direct heat with a cast iron grate installed. In a small saucepot, sauté shallots in a bit of butter. Add BBQ spice and then flambé with bourbon. Add a squeeze of lemon and then reserve sauce for when the oysters open. Place oysters on grill with the cup of the oyster flame side down. Put lid down and cook until they just pop open, about 5 minutes. When oysters open and they will stick to the top shell, shuck then into your bourbon pan sauce. Add a little of the oyster liqueur as well. Take a pair of kitchen scissors and cut the oysters in half or into bite size pieces. Place oysters back into the bottom shell and when ready re-fire on the grill Garnish with sliced chives, a pinch of BBQ spice and a little something crispy!

Raspberry Glazed Salmon

Servings:4

Cooking Time: 28 Minutes

Ingredients:

- Cedar grilling plank
- Fresh salmon fillet
- Raspberry BBQ Sauce

Directions:

1. Place the cedar plank in a pan, cover with water and soak for 2 hours. Coat salmon with raspberry BBQ sauce and let marinate for 2 hours.
2. Preheat the grill to 350°F using direct heat with a cast iron grate installed.
3. Place plank on cooking grid, close the dome and heat for about 3 minutes. Flip plank, using tongs, and place salmon on heated side of plank. Close dome and cook for 20-25 minutes.

Green Tomato Pizza With Smoked Chicken And Truffle Crema

Servings:8

Cooking Time: 10 Minutes

Ingredients:

- 8 oz (227 g) smoked chicken or turkey, pulled
- ½ red bell pepper, slivered
- 8 oz (227 g) fresh mozzarella cheese, cut into thin slices
- 2 tbsp (30 ml) fresh corn kernels (drain well if using canned)
- 4 or 5 fresh basil leaves, lightly chopped
- 1 cup (240 ml) warm water
- 1 tsp (5 ml) sugar
- 1 tsp (5 ml) active dry yeast
- 3 cups (710 ml) all-purpose flour
- 1½ tsp (8 ml) kosher salt
- ½ tsp (3 ml) dried Italian seasoning (optional)
- 2 tsp (10 ml) olive oil, divided
- 2 tbsp (30 ml) olive oil
- 5 medium green tomatoes
- ½ cup (120 ml) thinly sliced sweet or white onion
- 2 cloves garlic, minced
- 1 tsp (5 ml) kosher salt
- ½ tsp (3 ml) freshly ground black pepper
- 1 tsp (5 ml) sugar
- 1 tbsp (15 ml) white vinegar
- 2 tsp (10 ml) hot red pepper flakes
- ¼ cup (60 ml) fresh basil leaves, roughly chopped
- 1 tsp (5 ml) diced fresh oregano
- ½ cup (120 ml) crema
- 1½ tsp (8 ml) white truffle olive oil

Directions:

1. Run warm water until it is around 110°F, then measure 1 cup (240 ml) into a small bowl. Add the sugar and whisk, then sprinkle in the yeast and let sit until it blooms, 5 to 10 minutes.

2. With a stand mixer, mix together the flour, salt and Italian seasoning. Pour in the water/yeast and blend on low speed until combined. Add 1 tsp (5ml) of the olive oil and continue to blend until a dough forms, then keep mixing for 5 or 6 minutes. Lightly flour a Dough Rolling Mat, dump the dough onto it, and form into a ball. Drizzle the remaining teaspoon of olive oil into a large mixing bowl to coat the inside of the bowl. Transfer the dough ball to the bowl, cover with a damp towel, and let rise until it doubles in size, about 1½ hours.

3. While the dough is rising, prepare the sauce. Use 1 tsp (5 ml) of the olive oil to lightly oil the green tomatoes and char on the kamado grill, then set aside. In a small stockpot over medium heat, heat the remaining olive oil, add the onion and cook until softened, 3 to 4 minutes. Then add the garlic and cook for 2 minutes. Core and chop the tomatoes and add them along with the salt, pepper, sugar, vinegar and red pepper. Cook for 5 minutes, then decrease the heat and simmer for 25 to 30 minutes, stirring occasionally, until the tomatoes are soft. Stir in the basil and oregano, then, using an immersion blender (or food processor), blend until smooth.

4. To make the truffle crema, whisk the crema and truffle oil together. Store covered in the refrigerator until needed.

5. When the dough has risen, place on a lightly floured Dough Rolling Mat and knead 4 or 5 times, then divide into 4 parts. Roll out each piece into a 10 in (25 cm) circle (the thinner the better).

6. To assemble, spoon ½ cup (120 ml) sauce onto each crust and spread with the bottom of a spoon. Lay fresh mozzarella cheese on the pizza, then sprinkle smoked chicken, red bell pepper and fresh corn kernels over the pizzas.

7. Preheat the grill to 600°F using direct heat with a cast iron grate installed. Add a Pizza & Baking Stone. Dust a Pizza Peel with cornmeal, add a pizza, and slide onto the Stone for 5 to 6 minutes, or until the crust is browned and any cheese is melted. Remove and drizzle the Truffle Crema over the pizza, using a fork. Then sprinkle on the basil and serve.

Matt Barry Wings

Servings:12

Cooking Time: 30 Minutes

Ingredients:

- 3 dozen Springer Mountain Farms Chicken Wings
- 1 cup granulated garlic
- 1 cup kosher salt
- 1 cup white sugar
- 1 tbsp black pepper
- 1 tbsp cayenne
- ¼ cup paprika
- 1 tbsp chili pepper
- 1 tbsp guchang spice
- 1 tbsp bourbon molasses

Directions:

1. Blend spices thoroughly, keep them dry, cool and away from moisture. Toss the wings with an even distribution of spice.
2. Preheat the grill to 375°F using direct heat with a cast iron grate installed. Cook for about 30 minutes, turning occasionally, until the internal temperature reached 165°F or higher.

Polynesian Duck Kabobs

Servings:8

Cooking Time: 15 Minutes

Ingredients:

- 6- 7.5 oz Maple Leaf Farms Boneless Duck Breast Filets, thawed if frozen
- Salt and fresh ground black pepper, to taste
- 1 ripe fresh pineapple, peeled and cored
- 2 large red or yellow bell peppers, or one of each
- 2 large green bell peppers
- 2 small red onions
- 2⁄3 cup pineapple preserves
- 3 tablespoons dijon mustard

Directions:

1. Preheat the grill to 350°F using direct heat with a cast iron grate installed.
2. Remove skin from duck breasts. Cut duck breast into 2 inch chunks; season with salt and pepper to taste.
3. Cut pineapple into 11⁄2 inch chunks. Cut bell peppers into 11⁄2 inch chunks, discarding stems and seeds. Cut onions through the core into 1⁄2 inch thick wedges. Alternately thread duck, pineapple, bell peppers and onions onto Flexible Skewers.
4. Combine preserves and mustard; mix well. Arrange duck kabobs on kamado grill. Brush half of preserve mixture over kabobs. Grill covered 5 minutes. Turn; brush remaining half of preserve mixture over kabobs. Continue grilling covered 5 to 6 minutes or until duck is barely pink in center and peppers are crisp-tender.

Tandoori Chicken

Servings:4

Cooking Time: 30 Minutes

Ingredients:

- 4 bone-in skinless chicken breasts or thighs
- ½ cup plain Greek yogurt
- 1 lime, juiced
- 1 tbsp garam masala
- 4 cloves garlic, finely grated
- 1 inch of fresh ginger, finely grated
- ½ tbsp dry ginger powder
- ½ tbsp red chili powder
- ¼ tbsp cayenne pepper
- ½ tsp ground nutmeg
- ½ tbsp crushed fenugreek leaves
- ½ tbsp salt
- ¼ tsp red food color (Optional)

Directions:

1. One day before cooking, add all ingredients except the chicken in a bowl, and stir until combined. Make deep slashes in chicken and pour marinade over top. Massage the chicken to ensure all sides are coated. Marinade in the fridge for the flavors to deepen.

2. Preheat the grill to 400°F using direct heat with a cast iron grate installed.

3. Place Chicken onto the grill, bone side down. Cook for approximately 15 minutes per side or until chicken reaches and internal temperature of 165°F.

4. Serve with sweet white onions, warm naan and basmati rice.

Grilled Chicken Flat Bread With Taylor Farms Sweet Kale Salad

Servings:4

Cooking Time: 15 Minutes

Ingredients:

- 1 loaf of ciabatta bread
- 1 boneless, skinless chicken breast
- Savory Pecan Seasoning
- 1 tomato, sliced
- 1 ball of mozzarella, sliced
- 1 Tbsp olive oil
- Salt and pepper to taste
- 1 Taylor Farms Sweet Kale Chopped Kit

Directions:

1. Preheat the grill to 400°F using direct heat with a cast iron grate installed.

2. Season the chicken breast on both sides with the Savory Pecan Seasoning. Place on the grid and cook for 10 minutes per side or until the internal temperature reaches 165°F. Remove the chicken from the grill, slice, and set aside

3. Mix together the Taylor Farms Sweet Kale Chopped Kit and set aside.

4. Slice the ciabatta bread in the middle, lengthwise. Brush the olive oil on the sliced side of the bread and season with the salt and pepper. Place on the bread sliced-side down on the kamado grill for 3-5 minutes, or until desired grill marks appear.

5. Flip the bread and top with the mozzarella. Let cook for 3-5 minutes or until the mozzarella is melting; add tomatoes and cook for 3-5 minutes to desired doneness. Carefully remove from the kamado grill. Add chicken and top with the Taylor Farms Sweet Kale Chopped salad.

Hatch Chile Salsa And Chicken Casserole

Servings:6

Cooking Time: 55 Minutes

Ingredients:

- 5 boneless, skinless chicken breasts
- 32 oz. shredded cheddar cheese
- 32 oz. chicken stock
- 5-6 large tortillas
- ¼ cup Cotija cheese
- 15-20 Hatch chiles
- 1 small onion or ½ large onion
- 4 cloves garlic
- 1 bunch cilantro
- 1 tsp cumin
- ½ tsp coriander
- 2 limes, juiced
- 2 tsp honey
- Salt to taste

Directions:

1. Preheat the grill to 400°F using direct heat with a cast iron grate installed.

2. In the dutch oven, cover the chicken with chicken broth and 2 tbsp of the hatch chile salsa. Place on the grill and simmer until the internal temperature reaches 165°F, about 15 minutes. Remove from the grill, strain and chop the chicken.

3. In the same dutch oven, spread a tablespoon of salsa on the bottom. Next place a tortilla and top with chicken and a handful of cheese. Repeat this process until the ingredients are gone. Place on the grill and bake for 20 minutes or until the cheese is melted. During the last 5 minutes top with the Cotija cheese. Remove from the kamado grill and let rest for 10-15 minutes. Enjoy!

4. Preheat the grill to 400°F using direct heat with a cast iron grate installed.

5. Roast the Hatch chiles for 5 minutes per side or until there is a charred outside. Remove the chiles from the grill and place in a gallon-sized resealable bag for 10-15 minutes. The chiles should be soft and pliable at this point. Remove the skins, stems and seeds from the chiles.

6. To give the salsa even more of a roasted flavor you can also roast the onion, garlic and lime, however, this is an optional step. Put all the ingredients for the salsa in a blender or a food processor and blend together to desired consistency. Set aside.

Duck And Mango Quesadilla

Servings:24

Cooking Time: 10 Minutes

Ingredients:

- 1 Maple Leaf Farms duck breast*
- ½ cup mango, julienne
- 1 tbsp minced green onion
- 1 tbsp minced cilantro
- 1 tbsp sliced jalapenos, seeded
- 4 oz fresh mozzarella, julienne
- 6 flour tortillas, 6"

Directions:

1. Preheat the grill to 350°F using direct heat with a cast iron grate installed.
2. Grill duck breasts on kamado grill for 6 minutes, turning every 2 minutes. Remove skin and shred or cut meat into julienne strips.
3. Evenly divide cheese over bottom half of flour tortillas. Top each evenly with remaining ingredients.
4. Fold each tortilla in half. Gently press down to seal.
5. Grill tortillas on the kamado grill, 2-3 minutes per side until lightly golden.
6. Cut each tortilla into 4 wedges.
7. Roasted Garlic Marinated Duck Breast also works in this recipe.

Buffa-que Wings

Servings:16
Cooking Time: 40 Minutes

Ingredients:

- 16 whole chicken wings (about 3-1/2 pounds)
- 1/2 cup Tabasco sauce or your favorite hot sauce
- 1/2 cup fresh lemon juice
- 1/4 cup vegetable oil
- 2 tablespoons Worcestershire sauce
- 4 cloves garlic, minced
- 2 teaspoons coarse salt (kosher or sea)
- 1 teaspoon freshly ground black pepper
- 1-1/2 cups wood chips or chunks (preferably hickory or oak), soaked for 1 hour in water to cover, then drained
- 8 tablespoons (1 stick) salted butter
- 1/2 cup Tabasco sauce or your favorite hot sauce
- 4 ounces Maytag Blue cheese
- 1 cup mayonnaise
- 1/2 cup sour cream
- 1 tablespoon distilled white vinegar
- 1/4 cup minced onion
- 1/2 teaspoon freshly ground black pepper
- Coarse salt (kosher or sea; optional)

Directions:

1. Rinse the chicken wings under cold running water and blot them dry with paper towels. Cut the tips off the wings and discard them (or leave the tips on if you don't mind munching a morsel that's mostly skin and bones.) Cut each wing into 2 pieces through the joint.
2. Make the marinade: Whisk together the hot sauce, lemon juice, oil, Worcestershire sauce, garlic, salt and pepper in a large nonreactive mixing bowl. Stir in the wing pieces and let marinate in the refrigerator, covered, for 4 to 6 hours or as along as overnight, turning the wings several times so that they marinade evenly.
3. Make the mop sauce: Just before setting up the grill, melt the butter in a small saucepan over medium heat and stir in the hot sauce.
4. Toss wood chips or chunks in the kamado grill. Preheat the grill to 350°F using direct heat with a cast iron grate installed.
5. When ready to cook, drain the marinade off the wings and discard the marinade. Brush and oil the grid. Place the wings in the center of the hot grate, over the drip pan and away from the heat, and cover the grill. Cook the wings until the skin is crisp and golden brown and the meat is cooked through, 30 to 40 minutes. During the last 10 minutes, start blasting the wings with some of the mop sauce.
6. Transfer the grilled wings to a shallow bowl or platter and pour the remaining mop sauce over them. Serve with Maytag Blue Cheese Sauce and celery for dipping and of course plenty of paper napkins and cold beer.
7. Press the blue cheese through a sieve into a nonreactive mixing bowl.
8. Whisk in the mayonnaise, sour cream, vinegar, onion, and pepper. It's unlikely you'll need salt (the cheese is quite salty already) but taste for seasoning and add a little if necessary. The blue cheese sauce will keep in the refrigerator, covered, for several days.

Smoked Spanish Chicken

Servings:8

Cooking Time: 180 Minutes

Ingredients:

- 4-5lb all natural whole chicken
- 4 oz fresh chorizo sausage
- 1 can Landshark Lager
- 1 dried ancho chili
- 1 small lime, cut into 8 wedges
- 1 tsp whole black peppercorns
- 1 tsp smoked sweet paprika
- 1/2 tsp cumin
- 1/2 tsp chili powder
- 1 tsp cayenne pepper
- 1 1/2 tsp granulated garlic
- 1 1/2 tsp onion powder
- 2 tbs sea salt
- 1 tbs fresh ground black pepper
- 2 tablespoons of olive oil

Directions:

1. Pop open a can of Landshark and empty about half the liquid (Rusty recommends taking a few sips). Remove the pop-top and fill can with lime slices, onion and dried ancho peppers, seeds and all. Add black peppercorns and shake can.

2. Pat and dry chicken. Stuff most of the chorizo underneath the skin of the chicken. Take the last bit of chorizo and stuff in the neck area; it will self-baste as the chicken roasts.

3. Mix together cayenne pepper, cumin, garlic, powdered onion, paprika, chili powder, salt and pepper. Press and rub onto the skin of the chicken. Place Landshark can inside the chicken carcass and stand it up in foil pan to contain the drippings.

4. Place foil pan on the cooking grid of the kamado grill (you can smoke with apple or cherry wood for extra flavor) and cook for 2-1/2 to 2-3/4 hours at temperature of 315 to 325°F. Use a meat thermometer to thoroughly cook chicken. Remove beer can, let chicken rest for about 15 minutes and cut in half. Serve with fresh vegetables or green salad, and enjoy, compliments of Chef Rusty!

Salsa Verde Chicken Pasta

Servings:6

Cooking Time: 45 Minutes

Ingredients:

- 3 boneless, skinless chicken breasts, cubed
- 1½ tbsp olive oil
- 3 tomatillos, chopped
- 1 large white onion, chopped
- 1 large red bell pepper, chopped
- 1½ tsp paprika
- Salt and pepper to taste
- 3 cups uncooked rigatoni or rotini pasta
- 2¼ cups chicken broth (low sodium)
- 1½ cups salsa verde
- 4 tbsp chopped cilantro (save more for garnish)
- 5 ounces cream cheese
- 1 lime, juiced
- Diced avocado for topping

Directions:

1. Preheat the grill to 350°F using direct heat with a cast iron grate installed.
2. Preheat a Cast Iron Skillet for 5 minutes. Add the olive oil, tomatillos, onions and peppers and cook for 5 minutes, stirring occasionally.
3. Season the chicken with the paprika, salt and pepper; add to the skillet and cook for another 5 minutes.
4. Add the uncooked pasta, broth, salsa and cilantro. Cook for 25-30 minutes until the pasta is cooked through and the liquid is reduced; swirl in the cream cheese until melted. Remove from the kamado grill and stir in the lime juice.
5. Top with diced avocado and cilantro

Jerk Chicken Drums

Servings: 8

Cooking Time: 40 Minutes

Ingredients:

- 3 lbs chicken drumsticks
- 1 recipe Habanero Rub
- 1/4 cup olive oil
- The juice of two limes

Directions:

1. In a large zip top bag, combine Habanero Rub with olive oil and lime juice. Add chicken and refrigerate 4 hours or overnight.
2. Remove from fridge and allow to come to room temperature for 15 minutes.
3. Grilling:
4. Preheat the grill to 400°F using direct heat with a cast iron grate installed.
5. Shake off any excess marinade and place on the grid of the grill.
6. Close the dome and cook for 20 minutes.
7. Turn drumsticks and close the dome for an additional 15 minutes or until the juices run clear.

Chicken Sausage Southwest Surprise

Servings:4

Cooking Time: 10 Minutes

Ingredients:

- ½ cup tomatoes, diced
- 2 tablespoons bell pepper, diced
- 2 tablespoons onion, diced
- 1 tablespoon cilantro, minced
- ½ cup vegetable oil
- ⅛ teaspoon salt
- 1 tablespoon jalapeno pepper
- ⅓ cup black beans, rinsed and drained
- 4 Hoagie rolls
- 1 package of 12 ounce Johnsonville Chopotle Montery Jack Cheese Chicken Sausage, sliced
- 2 small tomatoes, sliced
- 2 jalapenos, sliced and grilled
- Additional cilantro

Directions:

1. Preheat the grill to 350°F using direct heat with a cast iron grate installed.

2. Combine all ingredients in a bowl; mix well.

3. Place chicken sausage on the kamado grill and cook evenly.

4. Cut bun to create a hinge. Lightly butter top and bottom of the bun. Place on the kamado grill, buttered side down. Grill for 30 seconds or until lightly browned. Remove roll from kamado grill.

5. Place two half slices of cheese on the bottom side of each bun. Top with ¼ cup of salsa. Place chicken sausage on salsa, top with sliced tomatoes and grilled sliced jalapenos. Sprinkle with additional cilantro.

O'neill Williams' Turkey Parmesan

Servings:4

Cooking Time: 35 Minutes

Ingredients:

- 2 egg whites
- 1 Tbsp water
- ½ cup Italian-seasoned dry bread crumbs
- 2 Tbsp freshly grated Parmesan cheese
- 1 lb. boneless turkey breast fillets (chicken can be used)
- 1 cup Italian-flavored tomato sauce
- 1 cup shredded mozzarella cheese

Directions:

1. Preheat the grill to 400°F using direct heat with a cast iron grate installed.

2. In a shallow bowl, beat egg whites with water. In another shallow bowl, combine bread crumbs and Parmesan cheese. Dip turkey into egg whites and then dredge in bread crumb mixture; place in a 13 X 9 pan.

3. Place pan on the cooking grid and bake 30 minutes. Pour tomato sauce evenly over the turkey and top with mozzarella cheese.

4. Bake 5 more minutes or until turkey is cooked through.

Stuffed Caprese Chicken Sandwich

Servings:4

Cooking Time: 14 Minutes

Ingredients:

- 2 cups balsamic vinegar
- 3 tablespoons honey
- 4 large boneless skinless chicken breasts
- salt, pepper, and garlic powder to taste
- 4 large slices tomato
- 8 small slices fresh whole milk mozzarella
- 8 large leaves fresh basil
- 4 Cobblestone Bread Co hamburger buns (Sesame Twist works great)

Directions:

1. In a small saucepan, heat the vinegar and honey over medium/high heat (375-450°F). Bring to a boil and then reduce to a simmer, stirring regularly. When it starts to thicken and has reduced by about half (approximately 10 minutes), remove from the heat and set aside.

2. Season each chicken breast with salt, pepper, and garlic powder to taste. Cut each breast lengthwise, but not all the way, forming a "pita" shape. This is where you will place the mozzarella, basil, and tomato later.

3. Place the chicken in two large ziplock bags and pour some of the balsamic reduction into each bag, reserving a small amount for garnish. Allow to marinate in the fridge for at least 30 minutes before grilling.

4. When ready to grill, spray your cooking grid with non-stick spray or brush with canola oil. Stuff each chicken with one slice tomato, 2 leaves basil, and 2 slices fresh mozzarella. Use a toothpick to seal the opening if desired, this will make flipping the chicken easier.

5. Grill the chicken over medium/high heat, approximately 450°F, for 5-7 minutes on each side or until chicken is cooked through. This will bed determined based on the thickness of the chicken you picked. When the chicken is white throughout, it's done!

6. Place chicken onto the bottom bun and drizzle with a bit more of the reserved balsamic reduction. Top with the top part of the bun. Enjoy!

Classic Hot Wings

Servings: 3

Cooking Time: 30 Minutes

Ingredients:

- 3-4 pounds chicken wings
- 1/4 cup Cajun Dry Rub
- 2 cups Frank's Buffalo Sauce

Directions:

1. Liberally sprinkle the wings with the Cajun Dry Rub
2. Grilling:
3. Preheat the grill to 400°F using direct heat with a cast iron grate installed.
4. Place the wings on the grid with the dome closed for 20-30 minutes, turning once halfway through cooking.
5. When the juices run clear, place the wings in a large bowl and pour the Franks Buffalo Sauce over them. Toss to coat.
6. Replace the wings on the grid and close all of the vents. Allow the wings to finish for 5 minutes.
7. Toss in the sauce once more and serve.

Spicy Bourbon Barrel Bbq Wings

Servings:12

Cooking Time: 150 Minutes

Ingredients:

- 3 dozen Springer Mountain Farms Chicken Wings
- 1 liter bourbon
- 4 cups brown sugar
- 1 yellow onion, chopped
- 2 cups dark molasses
- 1 quart ketchup
- 1 cup Worcestershire Sauce
- ½ cup whole fresh garlic
- ½ cup chopped chipotle peppers
- 1 whole bunch, not chopped thyme
- 3 tablespoon Liquid Smoke
- 1 cup honey
- 2 cups Dijon mustard
- 2 oranges, cut in quarters
- Salt to taste

Directions:

1. Combine all ingredients for the sauce in a large stock box and let simmer on low heat for 2 hours, then remove oranges, thyme, and onions. Blend the sauce until smooth, then pour through a strainer. Toss the chicken in the sauce and drain extra sauce.
2. Preheat the grill to 375°F using direct heat with a cast iron grate installed. Cook for about 30 minutes, turning occasionally, until the internal temperature reaches 165°F or higher.

Vidalia Onion And Sriracha-glazed Nashville Hot Wings

Servings:4

Cooking Time: 35 Minutes

Ingredients:

- 1 pound whole chicken wings
- 1 tbsp olive oil
- Nashville Hot Seasoning, to taste
- ½ bottle of Vidalia Onion and Sriracha Sauce

Directions:

1. Preheat the grill to 350°F using direct heat with a cast iron grate installed.
2. Separate the flats from the drumettes, discarding the wing tips. Coat with the olive oil and a generous amount of the Nashville Hot Seasoning.
3. Place the wings skin-side down on the grid and cook for 15 minutes. Flip the wings after 15 minutes and cook for another 15-20 minutes, or until the wings measure 175°F internally. Remove the wings and place in a bowl.
4. Pour in ½ bottle of the Vidalia Onion and Sriracha Sauce and stir to coat the wings while they are still hot. Serve and enjoy!

Wild Rice Turkey Biryani Stuffed Whole Pumpkin

Servings:12

Cooking Time: 40 Minutes

Ingredients:

- 1 large sugar pumpkin (approx. 3-4 pounds)
- 6 tbsp clarified butter
- 2 sweet onions, chopped
- 3 cloves garlic, minced
- 1 tsp fresh ginger, minced
- 10 green cardamom pods
- 3 whole cinnamon sticks
- ¼ tsp ground cloves
- ¼ tsp chili powder
- 1 tsp ground cumin
- 1 tsp ground coriander
- ½ tsp ground black pepper
- 1 cup wild rice
- 1 cup basmati rice, rinsed until clear water
- 2 lbs. ground turkey or chicken, cooked and browned
- 1 lemon
- 1 cup Craisins
- 1 cup tart apple (Granny Smith), diced
- ¾ cup pecans, toasted and chopped
- Coconut Oil
- Dizzy Pig Curry-ish
- 4 cups water

Directions:

1. Prepare Pumpkin:
2. Wash and dry the pumpkin.
3. Slice the top off the pumpkin using a sharp knife.
4. Remove the seeds and stringy center. Save the seeds for later.
5. Rub the inside of the pumpkin with melted coconut oil and Dizzy Pig Curry-ish.
6. Prepare Biryani (can be made a day ahead):
7. Melt the butter in a dutch oven.
8. Add the chopped onion and cook until browned.
9. Add garlic and ginger and next 7 ingredients. Saute until the spices "bloom", but careful not to burn.
10. Add the wild rice and basmati rice and mix well.
11. Add the water to the rice mixture and bring to a boil, cover and simmer for 30 minutes or until all of the liquid has been absorbed. Remove from heat.
12. Remove cinnamon sticks and cardamom pods from mixture.
13. Add the turkey, juice of 1 lemon, Craisins, apple and pecans.
14. Prepare Egg & Pumpkin:
15. Preheat the grill to 325°F using direct heat with a cast iron grate installed.
16. Place pumpkin in a pie plate.
17. Fill pumpkin to top with Biryani and place pumpkin lid on top.

18. Place pumpkin in pie plate on the platesetter – preferable to use the egg "feet" to raise it off the platesetter, but can be put directly on it.

19. Close lid of the egg and be sure that the stem of the pumpkin clears the hole on the Egg lid and that the temperature gauge does not pierce the flesh of the Egg.

20. Roast the pumpkin for 40 minutes or until a toothpick or knife can be inserted with minimal resistance. It should be the consistency of a cooked baked potato.

21. Remove from Egg and allow to rest with the top on for at least 10 minutes.

22. To Serve:

23. Scoop out the Biryani, ensuring to scoop the roasted pumpkin in the serving. Enjoy!

Dry Rub Smoked Chicken Wings With Buttermilk "berliner Weisse" Ranch

Servings:12

Cooking Time: 240 Minutes

Ingredients:

- 3 dozen Springer Mountain Farms Chicken Wings
- 3 quart water
- ¾ lb. brown sugar
- ¾ lb. kosher salt
- 10½ oz fresh ginger
- ¾ oz coriander seeds
- ¾ oz cloves
- ¾ oz white peppercorns
- ¾ oz whole allspice
- ¾ oz mustard seeds
- 1 grapefruit
- 1 lemon, cut in ¼
- 1 lime, cut in ¼
- 1 orange, cut in ¼
- 6 tbsp brown sugar
- 3 tbsp garlic powder
- 3 tbsp onion powder
- 3 tbsp celery salt
- 3 tbsp smoked paprika
- 1½ tbsp ground cumin
- 1½ tbsp salt
- 1½ tsp mustard powder
- 3 tbsp dry sage
- 3 tbsp white pepper
- 1½ tsp ground bay leaves
- 1½ tsp cayenne pepper
- 2 ¼ cup buttermilk
- ¾ cup sour cream
- 6 tablespoons beer "preferably Berliner weisse beer"
- 2¼ teaspoon apple cider vinegar
- ¾ teaspoon salt
- ¾ teaspoon black pepper
- 1 teaspoon of dry dill
- ¼ teaspoon dried parsley
- 1½ teaspoon dried oregano

Directions:

1. Remove the chicken wings from the brine and season with the Rub. Let them set for at least one hour.

2. Preheat the grill to 250°F using direct heat with a cast iron grate installed. Cook the wings for 3 to 4 hours, turning occasionally, until the internal temperature reaches 165°F or higher.

3. Served with Buttermilk "Berliner Weisse" Ranch.

4. Mix all brine ingredients with the exception of the citrus and the fresh thyme in a large pot. Bring to boil. After boiling, ice down the mixture and add the citrus and the fresh thyme. Cover the wings with the citrus brine and refrigerate overnight.

5. For the rub, mix all of the ingredients and preserve in a dry container.

6. For the ranch dressing, mix all the ingredients and let it rest in the refrigerator at least one hour before serving.

Braised Chicken Thighs With Mushrooms

Servings: 4

Cooking Time: 60 Minutes

Ingredients:
- 2 lbs chicken thighs, bone in and skin on
- 1 lb mushrooms, thinly sliced
- 1 cup finely chopped onion
- 1 Tablespoon butter
- 1 Tablespoon fresh thyme, chopped
- 1/2 cup white wine
- 1/2 cup chicken broth
- 1/4 cup flour
- 2 Tablespoons olive oil
- Salt and Pepper

Directions:
1. Lightly dredge each chicken thigh in flour and season with salt and pepper.
2. Preheat the grill to 500°F using direct heat with a cast iron grate installed.
3. Place the dutch oven directly on the grid and allow the pot to heat for 5-7 minutes.
4. Pour olive oil into the oven and add chicken thighs, being careful not to crowd the pan.
5. Brown the chicken thighs in batches until they are golden brown on all sides. Remove from the dutch oven and set aside.
6. To the pan, add butter and mushrooms, but do not stir for 2-3 minutes or until the mushrooms begin to brown.
7. Add onions and cook until softened.
8. Return the chicken to the pot and add wine, chicken, broth, and thyme.
9. Cover the dutch oven, reduce the heat of The grill to 350°F and close the dome.
10. Allow the chicken to cook 30-40 minutes or until the internal temperature reaches 170°F. Serve warm.

Roasted Chicken With Lemon And Garlic

Servings:8
Cooking Time: 80 Minutes

Ingredients:
- 1 chicken 3 1⁄2 to 4 lbs (1.5 to 1.8 kg), preferably organic
- Coarse salt (kosher or sea) and freshly ground black pepper
- 1 head garlic, cut in half crosswise
- 1 lemon, cut in half crosswise
- 3 sprigs fresh rosemary (optional)
- 1 tbsp (15 ml) extra virgin olive oil or butter, at room temperature

Directions:
1. Preheat the grill to 400°F using direct heat with a cast iron grate installed.
2. Rinse the chicken under cold water and blot dry with paper towels. Place the chicken in a Roasting & Drip Pan. Generously season the neck and cavities with salt and pepper. Place 2 garlic cloves in the main cavity along with 1 of the lemon halves and a sprig of rosemary. Place a third garlic clove in the neck cavity.
3. Concentrating on the breast, rub the chicken with the cut side of the garlic, remaining lemon half and the butter or olive oil. Generously season the bird on all sides with salt and pepper. Truss the chicken, then place breast side up in the pan. Add the garlic halves, lemon half and rosemary, with the cut side of the garlic and lemon facing the bird.
4. Place the chicken in the kamado grill and roast it until the skin is crisp and golden brown and the meat is cooked through, 1 to 1 1⁄4 hours. After 30 minutes, start basting the bird with the juices that accumulate in the bottom of the pan.
5. Roast until the internal temperature reaches 165°F/74°C. Lay a piece of foil over the breast if it starts to brown too much before the bird is fully cooked.
6. Transfer the chicken to a cutting board and let it rest for about 5 minutes. Remove the trussing string before carving the bird.

Grilled Pheasant With Chimichurri

Servings: 4
Cooking Time: 30 Minutes

Ingredients:
- 2 pheasants (about 1 1/4 to 1 1/2 pounds each)
- 4 cups Turkey Brine
- 1 cup Chimichurri

Directions:
1. Cover pheasants with Turkey Brine and allow to sit a minimum of 2 hours or up to overnight.
2. Grilling:
3. Preheat the grill to 400°F using direct heat with a cast iron grate installed. Put the plate setter in place along with the grid.
4. Place the dried pheasants on the grid and cover for 30 minutes or until the internal temperature of the thigh reaches 160°F.
5. Remove the pheasants from the grill and cover with chimichurri. Serve.

Hop's Hawaiian Bbq Chicken Pizza

Servings:4

Cooking Time: 17 Minutes

Ingredients:

- 1 lb pizza dough
- 4 oz chopped chicken
- 2 oz chopped ham
- 4 oz chopped pineapple
- Your favorite BBQ sauce
- 1/4 cup shredded cheddar
- 1/2 cup shredded mozzarella

Directions:

1.   Preheat the grill to 550°F using direct heat with a cast iron grate installed.

2.   I soaked my chicken breast in pineapple juice and BBQ sauce for an hour before I threw it on the kamado grill. Once it was done, I chopped off what I needed for the pie and ate the rest.

3.   Next, I added the Pizza Stone, heat the stone before putting your pizza in the kamado grill. If you're good at making your own pizza dough, then you're ahead of me already. I got mine from the grocery store and rolled it out over a bed of finely ground corn meal so it doesn't stick to the counter; I prefer cornmeal to flour.

4.   Throw some corn meal on the hot stone in the kamado grill and place the dough on it, close the lid and cook the dough for about 2 minutes per side. This will make a crispier crust and will make it easier to handle with the ingredients on it.

5.   Remove the dough from the kamado grill and spread on the BBQ sauce. Now you're ready for the ham, chicken, pineapple and cheese. If you want more chicken, add more chicken. If you want more cheese, add more cheese. It's pizza, for crying out loud! Put the pie back into the kamado grill and cook it covered for 12-15 minutes or until properly browned.

Whole Turkey With Light Salt Brine

Servings:8

Cooking Time: 270 Minutes

Ingredients:

- One 12-14 pound turkey
- 1 tbsp crushed hot red pepper flakes
- 2 tbsp boiling water
- 18 cups water
- ½ cup kosher salt
- 1 tbsp granulated sugar
- 4 thyme sprigs, bruised with the broad side of a knife
- 2 tbsp black peppercorns, crushed with a dowel or bottom of a heavy pot
- Three .18 ounce packets Goya Sazón Azafran
- About ½ cup canola or vegetable oil
- 3 tbsp garlic salt
- 1 ½ tbsp chili powder
- 1 ½ tbsp coarsely ground fresh black pepper
- 8 tbsp (4 ounces) unsalted butter, melted
- ½ bunch thyme and ½ bunch sage tied in an herb bundle
- ½ cup extra virgin olive oil
- 6 tbsp finely chopped chives
- Fleur de sel
- Finely ground black pepper

Directions:

1. Place the pepper flakes in a small bowl and pour the boiling water over them; let sit for 1 to 2 minutes to rehydrate the flakes. Combine all the brine ingredients, including the pepper flakes and the soaking water in a large bowl and stir to dissolve the salt and sugar. Let sit at room temperature for 24 hours to allow the flavors to develop.

2. Place the turkey in a jumbo-sized resealable bag or a brining bag. Pour in the brine, squeeze out any excess air from the bag, and close. Place into another bag for insurance against leaking, and seal again. Refrigerate for at least 12 hours or up to 24. If you don't have room in your refrigerator the turkey can be stored in a small cooler with ice or frozen ice packs.

3. Preheat the grill to 275°F using direct heat with a cast iron grate installed with hickory or pecan chips. Remove the turkey from the bags; rinse and lightly pat dry with paper towels. Lightly coat the turkey with canola oil and place in a roasting rack with a drip pan. Place the turkey in the kamado grill and cook until the internal temperature of the thigh registers 160ºF and the breast registers 155ºF.

4. Meanwhile, combine the seasoning blend ingredients. Brush the skin or the turkey with the melted butter and season all of the skin with the seasoning blend.

5. Continue cooking until the turkey has reached a safe minimum internal temperature of 165°F throughout the product, about 3¾ hours to 4½ hours total, depending on the size of the bird.

6. Drizzle the olive oil on an extra-large cutting board. Top with the chives, fleur de sel, and pepper. Remove the turkey from the cooker, place on the board, and let rest for 15 minutes. Slice the breast and dredge in the dressing. Pull all of the dark meat from the thighs into chunks and dredge in the dressing. Leave the drumsticks and wings whole. Arrange on a serving plate and sprinkle with fleur de sel and pepper.

Chicken & Veggie Stir-fry

Servings:6

Cooking Time: 10 Minutes

Ingredients:

- 2 tablespoons toasted sesame oil
- 1½ teaspoons plus 1½ teaspoons minced garlic
- 1½ teaspoons plus 1½ teaspoons minced fresh ginger
- 2 pounds boneless, skinless chicken breasts, cubed
- ½ cup rice wine
- ½ cup light soy sauce
- ½ cup chicken stock
- ¼ cup hoisin sauce
- 2 tablespoons rice wine vinegar
- 2 tablespoons granulated sugar
- 2 tablespoons cornstarch
- 1 teaspoon chili garlic sauce (optional)
- ½ cup canola oil
- 4 cups broccoli florets
- 1 cup broccoli stems, trimmed and julienned
- 1 cup julienned carrots
- 1 cup drained water chestnuts, diced
- 1 tablespoon toasted sesame seeds

Directions:

1. Preheat the grill to 500°F using direct heat with a cast iron grate installed.

2. Combine the sesame oil, 1½ teaspoons of the garlic, and 1½ teaspoons of the ginger in a small bowl, add the chicken, and toss to coat. Let the chicken marinate for 30 minutes.

3. To make the sauce, mix the remaining 1½ teaspoons garlic, 1½ teaspoons ginger, rice wine, soy sauce, chicken stock, hoisin sauce, rice wine vinegar, sugar, cornstarch, and chili garlic sauce in a small bowl. Set aside.

4. Place a Carbon Steel Wok on the spander and preheat for 2 minutes.

5. Place the canola oil and chicken in the wok. Close the lid of the kamado grill and cook for 5 to 6 minutes, until seared on all sides. Add the broccoli florets and stems, carrots, and water chestnuts and cook for 2 to 3 minutes, stirring well. Add the sauce and continue to cook until the sauce has thickened. Remove the wok from the kamado grill.

6. Transfer the stir-fry to a bowl and garnish with the sesame seeds.

BURGERS

Breakfast Burger

Servings: 4

Cooking Time: 13 Minutes

Ingredients:

- 1 1/2 lb ground beef
- 1/2 lb ground pork breakfast sausage
- 2 Tablespoon butter
- 8 strips bacon
- 4 slices sharp cheddar cheese
- 4 Brioche buns
- 4 eggs
- 4 thick slices tomato

Directions:

1. In a medium bowl, mix ground beef and sausage until just combined.
2. Form into 4 patties and refrigerate while the grill heats.
3. Melt butter in a large skillet and fry the eggs for 2 minutes on each side.
4. Grilling:
5. Preheat the grill to 400°F using direct heat with a cast iron grate installed.
6. Place bacon on a small cookie sheet and place on the grid in the grill. Cook until crispy.
7. Place the patties on the grid and close the dome for 3 minutes.
8. Flip the burgers and replace the dome for an additional 3 minutes.
9. Close all of the vents and allow the burgers to sit for an additional 5 minutes. The internal temperature of the burger should be 150°F.
10. Place cheese on top of the burgers and cover for 1 more minute.
11. Assemble the burgers by placing a burger on the bottom bun, topping with bacon, tomato, and a fried egg.

Classic American Burger

Servings: 4
Cooking Time: 12 Minutes

Ingredients:
- 2 lbs ground beef
- 1/2 tsp salt
- 1/4 tsp pepper
- 4 slices American cheese
- 4 hamburger buns
- Green Leaf Lettuce
- Sliced Tomato
- Ketchup
- Mustard
- Sliced Pickle

Directions:
1. Form ground beef into four patties and season both sides with salt and pepper.
2. Grilling:
3. Preheat the grill to 500°F using direct heat with a cast iron grate installed.
4. Place burgers on the grid and close the dome for 3 minutes.
5. Flip burgers and close the dome for 2 more minutes.
6. Close all of the vents and allow the burgers to sit for 5 minutes.
7. Top each burger with a slice of cheese and close the dome for 1 more minute.
8. Build burgers with lettuce, tomato, pickle, mustard, and ketchup.

Oahu Burger

Servings: 4
Cooking Time: 12 Minutes

Ingredients:
- 2 lbs ground beef
- 1/4 cup thickened Teriyaki Marinade
- 1/4 cup mayonnaise
- 1/2 tsp sambal or sriracha
- 4 slices fresh pineapple, cored
- 4 slices tomato
- 4 slices butter lettuce
- 4 Hawaiian hamburger buns

Directions:
1. Form ground beef into four patties and season both sides with salt and pepper.
2. In a small bowl, mix mayonnaise with hot chile sauce and spread on buns.
3. Top each bun with a burger, slice of pineapple, lettuce and tomato.
4. Grilling:
5. Preheat the grill to 500°F using direct heat with a cast iron grate installed.
6. Place burgers on the grid and close the dome for 3 minutes.
7. Flip burgers, baste with Teriyaki Marinade, and place the pineapple slices on the grid. Close the dome for 2 more minutes.
8. Flip the burgers again and baste with remaining Teriyaki Marinade. Close the dome.
9. Close all of the vents and allow the burgers to sit for 5 minutes.

Quesadilla Burger

Servings: 4
Cooking Time: 12 Minutes

Ingredients:

- 2 lbs ground beef
- 2 Tablespoons Adobo Rub
- 1 cup shredded cheddar cheese
- 4 large flour tortillas
- Sour Cream
- Guacamole
- Salsa

Directions:

1. Form ground beef into four patties and season both sides with Adobo Rub.
2. Serve each burger with sour cream, guacamole, and salsa.
3. Grilling:
4. Preheat the grill to 500°F using direct heat with a cast iron grate installed.
5. Place burgers on the grid and close the dome for 3 minutes.
6. Flip burgers and close the dome for 2 more minutes.
7. Close all of the vents and allow the burgers to sit for 5 minutes.
8. Remove burgers and place flour tortillas on the grid.
9. Top each tortilla with shredded cheese and close the dome for 1 minute until the cheese melts.
10. Place a hamburger in the center of each tortilla and begin folding the tortilla around the burger like an envelope.

The Crowned Jewels Burger

Servings: 4
Cooking Time: 12 Minutes

Ingredients:

- 2 lbs ground beef
- 1/2 tsp salt
- 1/4 tsp pepper
- 1 lb thinly sliced pastrami
- 1 cup shredded Romaine lettuce
- 1/4 cup mayonnaise
- 2 Tablespoons ketchup
- 1/8 tsp onion powder
- 4 slices Sharp Cheddar cheese
- 4 hamburger buns
- 1 tomato, sliced

Directions:

1. Form ground beef into four patties and season both sides with salt and pepper.
2. Meanwhile, mix together mayonnaise, ketchup, and onion powder. Smear on each bun.
3. Place each pastrami and cheese covered burger on the prepared buns and top with shredded lettuce and tomato.
4. Grilling:
5. Preheat the grill to 500°F using direct heat with a cast iron grate installed.
6. Place burgers on the grid and close the dome for 3 minutes.
7. Flip burgers and close the dome for 2 more minutes.
8. Close all of the vents and allow the burgers to sit for 5 minutes.
9. Top each burger with 1/4 of the pastrami and a slice of cheese and close the dome for 1 more minute.

"the Masterpiece"

Servings: 4

Cooking Time: 12 Minutes

Ingredients:

- 2 lbs ground beef
- 6 ounces sliced mushrooms
- 4 Tablespoons shredded smoked Gouda
- 2 Tablespoons butter
- 2 Tablespoons olive oil
- 2 Tablespoons Dijon mustard
- 1/2 tsp salt
- 1/4 tsp pepper
- 8 slices bacon, cooked and crumbled
- 4 slices Swiss cheese
- 4 brioche buns
- 1 small onion, sliced

Directions:

1. Heat a skillet over medium heat and add 1 Tablespoon butter and 1 Tablespoon olive oil.
2. Place mushrooms in the pan and DO NOT MOVE THEM. Saute for 5-7 minutes or until the mushrooms are browned. Remove from the pan and set aside.
3. In the same skillet, heat remaining butter and olive oil and add onions. Saute over medium heat until they become translucent and begin to brown, about 10 minutes. Remove from the heat and set aside to cool.
4. Mix onion, mushrooms, and crumbled bacon.
5. Grilling:
6. Preheat the grill to 425°F using direct heat with a cast iron grate installed.
7. Form ground beef into eight patties and season both sides with salt and pepper.
8. Place a generous spoonful of the mushroom and onion mixture in the center of four patties and top with smoked Gouda.
9. Top with additional patty and press sides to seal the mixture inside.
10. Place burgers on the grid and close the dome for 5 minutes.
11. Flip burgers and close the dome for 3 more minutes.
12. Close all of the vents and allow the burgers to sit for 5 minutes.
13. Top each burger with a slice of Swiss cheese and close the dome for 1 more minute.
14. Spread buns with mustard, top with burgers and bun tops.

BEEF

Pulled Lamb Nachos

Servings:4

Cooking Time: 5 Minutes

Ingredients:

- 1 lamb shoulder, bone in
- 2/3 cup apple juice, hot
- 2 tbsp BBQ spice (your favorite)
- 3/4 lb. corn chips, preferably artisanal
- 1 cup of shredded mozzarella
- 1 cup of shredded cheddar cheese
- 10 cherry tomatoes, sliced
- 2 tbsp sliced Kalamata olives
- 1 jalapeno pepper, chopped
- 3 tbsp minced green onions
- ¼ cup chopped fresh coriander, as garnish
- 1/2 cup sour cream, to serve
- 1/2 cup salsa, to serve

Directions:

1. Preheat the grill to 250°F using direct heat with a cast iron grate installed.
2. Smoke the lamb shoulder for 4-5 hours until internal temperature reaches 195°F. Remove from the grill, cover with foil and rest for at least 30 minutes. Once cooled, pull the meat.
3. Mix together the apple juice and BBQ sauce. Cover the meat with the mixture.
4. Preheat the grill to 350°F using direct heat with a cast iron grate installed.
5. Place the tortilla chips on a round pan and top with cheese, pulled lamb, tomatoes, olives, and jalapeños. Put the pan on back on the kamado grill and cook for 5 minutes, or until cheese is fully melted.
6. Remove from the kamado grill and top with green onions and coriander. Serve with sour cream and salsa.

Grape And Hatch Chile Marinated Tri Tip

Servings:6

Cooking Time: 75 Minutes

Ingredients:

- 3½ cups red, green and black Moscato grapes, rinsed
- 2 tablespoons whole grain Dijon mustard
- 1/3 cup white wine vinegar
- ¾ cup Cognac
- ½ sweet onion, diced
- 3 New Mexico Hatch Chiles, roasted; peeled; stemmed and seeded
- 1 lime, juiced
- 1 green apple, cored; diced
- Kosher salt and freshly ground pepper, to taste
- 1 Tri Tip Roast

Directions:

1. Preheat the grill to 350°F using direct heat with a cast iron grate installed.

2. Place the first 9 ingredients into a sauce pan and bring to a boil. Reduce the heat and simmer for 30 minutes. Remove from the heat and using an immersion blender, carefully purée the mixture.

3. Place the Tri tip in a resealable bag. Pour the marinade over the meat and seal the bag. Marinate for one hour.

4. After one hour, place the meat in the rectangular drip pan and pour the marinade over the top. Bake for 35-45 minutes or until you reach your desired doneness.

Brisket Poutine

Servings:6

Cooking Time: 10 Minutes

Ingredients:

- One 10 to 12 lb (4.5 to 5.5 kg) whole packer brisket (Choice or higher)
- 1 cup (240 ml) coarsely ground pepper
- 1 cup (240 ml) non-iodized salt
- ¼ cup (60 ml) granulated garlic
- ¼ cup (60 ml) onion powder
- ¼ cup (60 ml) paprika
- French fries
- Cheese curds
- 6 Tbsp. unsalted butter
- ¼ cup unbleached all-purpose flour
- 20 oz. beef broth
- 10 oz. chicken broth
- Pepper, to taste

Directions:

1. Mix the rub ingredients in a large bowl. This mix will make more than you need for one brisket; store the remainder in an airtight container.

2. Trim the excess fat and silver skin from the brisket. Also, remove any "hard" pieces of fat as they will not render off during the cooking process. Trim the fat off the bottom of the brisket leaving only ¼ in (6 mm) fat. Apply rub to all sides of the meat liberally. Cover the brisket and place in the refrigerator to marinate overnight.

3. Preheat the grill to 250°F using direct heat with a cast iron grate installed.

4. Place the brisket on the grid, fat-side down – this is my preference, but highly debated in the barbecue world. Fat-side up is fine if that is your preference, but fat down is what many competitors do as it gives you a much better presentation. When the meat reaches an internal temperature of 160°F, double wrap the brisket in non-waxed butcher paper or aluminum foil – this is what we call the Texas crutch. The bark will have formed nicely by this point.

5. Continue to smoke the brisket until the meat is "probe tender," which means when you probe it there is no resistance. Each piece of meat is different but this will likely be at an internal temperature of between 200-202°F. Remove the brisket from the grill, wrap in a towel and place in a cooler for at least one hour. This will allow the juices to re-distribute in the meat. Unwrap the brisket and slice against the grain.

6. Prepare the gravy: In a small bowl, dissolve the cornstarch in the water and set aside. In a large saucepan, melt the butter. Add the flour to create the roux and cook, stirring regularly, for about 5 minutes, until the mixture turns golden brown. Add the beef and chicken broth and bring to a boil, stirring with a whisk. Stir in the cornstarch and simmer for 3 to 5 minutes or until the sauce thickens. Season to taste with salt and pepper. Prepare French fries, chop brisket. Top French fries with brisket, French fries, cheese curds, and gravy.

Tex Mex Burger

Servings:4

Cooking Time: 8 Minutes

Ingredients:

- 4 Nature's Own 100% Whole Wheat Sandwich Rolls 2 teaspoons fresh lime juice
- 1 teaspoon ground cumin
- 1 teaspoon chili powder
- 1/4 teaspoon salt
- 1/8 teaspoon black pepper
- Dash cayenne pepper
- 1 pound lean ground beef
- 4 slices Manchego, Chihuahua or Cheddar cheese 4 tablespoons sour cream
- Jalapeño pepper jelly

Directions:

1. Preheat the grill to 350°F using direct heat with a cast iron grate installed.
2. Combine lime juice, cumin, chili powder, salt, black pepper and cayenne pepper in a large bowl; mix well. Add beef; mix well. Form into 4 patties.
3. Cook about 4 minutes per side, adding cheese slices during the last 2 minutes of grilling.
4. Toast insides of sandwich rolls. Spread 1 tablespoon sour cream on each roll. Place burgers on roll bottoms. Garnish with jelly.

Smoked Goat Bolognese

Servings: 8
Cooking Time: 150 Minutes

Ingredients:

- 1½lb (680g) boneless goat leg
- kosher salt and freshly ground black pepper
- 1–2 tsp sweet smoked paprika
- 1 medium yellow onion, chopped
- 4 garlic cloves, chopped
- 3 celery stalks, diced
- 2 carrots, diced
- 1½ cups beer
- 1½ cups cola
- 1lb (450g) dried rigatoni
- olive oil
- for the sauce
- 1 tbsp olive oil
- 1 white onion, diced
- 4 garlic cloves, minced
- 15oz (425g) can crushed tomatoes
- 1 cup red wine
- 1 tsp fresh oregano, minced
- ½ cup heavy cream
- to smoke
- cherry or wine barrel wood chunks

Directions:

1. About 2 to 3 hours before cooking, coat goat leg liberally with salt, pepper, and a light (but thorough) dusting of paprika. Cover with plastic wrap and allow to come to room temperature.

2. Preheat the grill to 250°F (121°C). Once hot, add the wood chunks, then install the heat deflector and a standard grate with a dutch oven on the grate. Add onion, garlic, celery, and carrots to the dutch oven. Close the grill lid and sweat the vegetables for 5 minutes. Stir in beer and cola, and add goat leg.

3. Loosely cover the dutch oven with aluminum foil, close the grill lid, and smoke until the internal temperature reaches 190°F (88°C), about 1 to 2 hours, checking the temperature every hour. Transfer goat leg to a large serving platter and let rest for 30 to 45 minutes, then shred the meat. Season with salt and pepper to taste. Set aside.

4. Cook the rigatoni on the stovetop according to package directions. Drain and rinse with cold water, and toss with a little olive oil to prevent sticking. Set aside.

5. To make the sauce, on the stovetop in a large skillet over medium heat, heat oil until shimmering. Add onions and garlic, and sauté until fragrant and beginning to brown, about 2 to 3 minutes. Add tomatoes, wine, and oregano. Cook until reduced by one-fourth, about 10 to 15 minutes.

6. Add shredded meat, cream, and cooked rigatoni to the skillet. Stir gently and cook until thick, about 5 to 7 minutes. Season with salt and pepper to taste, and serve warm.

Smash Burgers

Servings: 16

Cooking Time: 8 Minutes

Ingredients:

- 2 tbsp unsalted butter
- 2 tbsp canola oil
- 1/2 cup minced shallots or red onion
- 2lb (1kg) ground chuck
- kosher salt and freshly ground black pepper
- 16 sweet Hawaiian rolls or slider buns
- 5oz (140g) Brie or cheese of choice, cut into 16 slices
- tomato slices, to serve
- dill pickle slices, to serve

Directions:

1. Preheat the grill to 400°F (204°C) using direct heat with a cast iron grate installed flat side up. To the hot griddle, add butter and canola oil. Make 8 small piles of half the shallots on the griddle, about 2 tsp per pile.

2. Portion ground beef into 16 balls, and season with salt and pepper to taste. Place one meatball on each pile of shallots. Using a spatula, smash the meat into the shallots, forming a thin patty.

3. Close the lid and grill the burgers until shallots begin to caramelize and the meat is cooked on the bottom, about 2 minutes. Don't move the patties. When the bottoms are caramelized, flip the burgers, being sure to get most of the shallots.

4. Place a slice of cheese on each patty and the top bun on the cheese. Leave in place on the griddle for 2 minutes. On a serving platter, top the bottom halves of the buns with tomato and pickle slices. Using a spatula, slide the burgers and top buns from the griddle and place atop the bottom buns. Repeat steps 2 through 4 with the remaining shallots, meat, and toppings. Serve immediately.

Grilled Italian Meatloaf Sandwich

Servings:4

Cooking Time: 140 Minutes

Ingredients:

- 2 pounds of 80% lean ground beef
- ½ cup shredded Parmesan cheese
- 1 tablespoon Worcestershire sauce
- ¼ cup of marinara sauce (save extra from the jar for brushing on top of the meatloaf)
- 1 cup of breadcrumbs
- ½ teaspoon black pepper
- ¾ teaspoon kosher salt
- 3 eggs
- 2 teaspoon red pepper flakes
- 2 tablespoons dried parsley
- 2 tablespoons dried basil
- 2 tablespoons dried oregano
- ½ cup of diced sweet onion
- 1 tablespoon of diced garlic
- ½ cup of minced carrots
- Cobblestone Bread Co (TM) Toasted Onions Rolls
- Sliced Mozzarella Cheese

Directions:

1. Lightly mix the ingredients together in a large bowl. Form the meatloaf on a grilling plank and let it rest a few minutes.

2. Preheat the grill to 350°F using direct heat with a cast iron grate installed. Cook for approximately 2 hours. With one hour left, take additional marinara sauce and brush it on top of the meatloaf. Repeat every 15-20 minutes until a nice tomato glaze has formed on top. The meatloaf is cooked when the meat registers 165°F in the center.

3. Let the meatloaf rest and cool a bit. Take the Cobblestone Bread Co (TM) Toasted Onion Rolls and lightly grill them for about 30 seconds to get warm. Slice the meatloaf thick and assemble the sandwich by placing the meatloaf on the roll and topping it with a slice of mozzarella cheese.

Bolognese

Servings: 6
Cooking Time: 90 Minutes

Ingredients:

- 2 lbs ground beef
- 4 oz bacon, diced
- 1 cup milk
- 2 cloves garlic
- 1 stalk celery
- 1 carrot
- 1 small onion
- 2 cups chicken broth
- 1 cup red wine
- 1/4 cup tomato paste
- 1 tsp Italian seasoning

Directions:

1. In the bowl of a food processor, combine celery, carrot, onion, and garlic and pulse until finely chopped.
2. Grilling:
3. Preheat the grill to 300°F using direct heat with a cast iron grate installed.
4. Place the bacon in a cold dutch oven and begin heating on the stove over medium heat.
5. Cook the bacon until it is crisp and the fat is rendered.
6. Remove all but 2 Tablespoon of the fat.
7. Add ground beef and cook until brown.
8. Add chopped vegetables and cook for 5 minutes.
9. Add tomato paste and cook for an additional 2 minutes.
10. Add milk and stir. Allow the liquid to evaporate until the milk solids are left behind.
11. Add wine, chicken broth, and Italian seasoning.
12. Cover the dutch oven and transfer it to the grill. Allow the sauce to cook for 1 hour before serving over pasta.

Steak Caramelized Onions

Servings:2
Cooking Time: 4 Minutes

Ingredients:

- 1 Shoulder steak
- 2 Tablespoons olive oil, separated
- 1 Medium white onion, sliced
- 1 Cup Miller LITE beer
- 1 Tablespoon Plugra unsalted butter
- Salt and pepper, to taste

Directions:

1. Preheat the grill to 450°F using direct heat with a cast iron grate installed. In the meantime, heat a large skillet over medium high heat and add to tablespoons of the oil and swirl to coat well. Add the sliced onions. Sauté the onions until caramelized (about 4 minutes). Add beer and simmer until liquid is reduced by 75%. Add the butter and swirl until melted. Set aside and keep warm.
2. Rub all sides of the steak with one tablespoon of oil and season to taste with the salt and pepper. Place on hot grill and sear for three minutes per side. Lower the heat and continue to cook; turning often until done to your liking. Remove the steaks from the grill and let them rest for 5-8 minutes.
3. Place the steak on serving plates and spoon caramelized onions over the top.

Smoked & Braised Beef Short Ribs

Servings:12

Cooking Time: 220 Minutes

Ingredients:

- 1 large head of cabbage, cut into 8 equal pieces
- 1/3 cup olive oil
- 1 tbsp kosher salt
- 1 tbsp crushed red pepper
- 4 medium size slicing tomatoes – cut lengthwise
- ¼ cup olive oil
- 1 tsp salt
- 1 tsp pepper
- 1 tbsp lemon juice
- 1 tsp crushed red pepper
- 8 single bone-in short ribs (about 8-10 ounces each)
- 1 medium yellow onions, diced
- 2 medium carrots, peeled and diced
- 1 head celery, diced – save rib and inner leaves
- 1 leak, sliced into 1" rings
- 4 garlic cloves, minced
- 1 shallot, minced
- ¼ cup Dijon mustard
- ¼ cup red wine vinegar
- 1 cup red wine
- Mixed aromatics and herbs – 2 bay leaves, 8 black pepper corns, 2 sprigs fresh thyme, 2 sprigs rosemary
- 3 cups beef stock
- 1 cup chicken stock
- ¼ cup canola oil
- Salt and pepper to taste

Directions:

1. Preheat the grill to 250°F using direct heat with a cast iron grate installed.

2. Heavily season the cabbage with olive oil, kosher salt and crushed red pepper. Place the 8 pieces of seasoned cabbage around the edge of a dutch oven, leaving space for the tomatoes. Place the tomato halves alternating with the cabbage.

3. Cook the tomatoes and cabbage. Remove the tomatoes after 1½ hours or once the skins can be easily removed; allow the tomatoes to cool. Cook the cabbage for another 3½ hours, removing the cabbage from the kamado grill when the heart of the cabbage can release from the center once gently pulled – reserve the cabbage for later.

4. Remove the tomato skins and crush the tomatoes into a pot, cooking on medium heat until simmer. Season the smoked tomatoes with lemon juice, salt and crushed red pepper, remove from heat and keep the tomatoes in the pot.

5. Remove the platesetter and set the kamado grill for direct cooking at 400°F/204°C.

6. Season the short ribs aggressively with salt and pepper. Sear evenly on all sides and remove from the grill. Heat the dutch oven (still direct cooking) with canola oil. Roast onions, carrots, celery, leeks in the

dutch oven, season with salt and pepper, and cook until the onions are translucent – about 8-10 minutes, stirring occasionally. Add garlic, shallot and aromatics and cook until shallots are translucent.

7. Add the mustard, stir and cook for two minutes, or until reduced. Add the red wine vinegar, stir and cook for two minutes or until reduced. Add the red wine, stir and cook for 4-5 minutes or until reduced. Add the beef and chicken stocks into the pot and bring to a simmer.

8. Place the seared short ribs back into the dutch oven and carefully remove the dutch oven from the grill.

9. Replace the platesetter and set the kamado grill for indirect cooking with the platesetter at 250°F.

10. Replace the dutch oven back to the grill. Place the cabbage slices and tomatoes around the edge of the dutch oven. Cook for 5 hours or until short ribs are tender.

Smoked Oxtail Stew

Servings:6

Cooking Time: 240 Minutes

Ingredients:

- 3.5 lbs Oxtails
- 4 stalks celery, medium chopped
- 2 onions, medium chopped
- 8 oz cremini mushrooms, halved
- 1 small butternut squash, medium chopped
- 4 carrots, medium chopped
- Olive oil, salt, pepper (to brown)
- 6 tsp all purpose flour
- 3 tsp Louisiana Hot Sauce
- 1 tbs Creole seasoning
- 1 tbs granulated garlic
- 1 tbs fresh garlic
- 3 tbs whole grain dijon mustard
- 4 cups beef stock
- 2 tbs soy sauce
- 3 tbs ketchup
- 3 sprigs rosemary
- 2 x 14 oz cans chopped tomatoes
- 2 tbs salt
- 2 tbs pepper
- Mesquite and cherry wood, soaked in water
- Deep roaster foil pain (about 12" x 10" x 4")

Directions:

1. Oil, salt, and pepper the oxtails; brown on the grill with the cooking grid only. Let oxtails rest after browning.

2. Preheat the grill to 350°F using direct heat with a cast iron grate installed.

3. Cut all vegetables. Mix stock, mustard, soy, ketchup, and tomatoes in separate bowl. Place all vegetables, herbs, tails, and flour in a bowl and toss. Place mixture in a deep roasting pan and add liquid. Place soaked wood on fire and smoke for 4 hours at 350°F. Halfway through, cover with foil and stop adding wood.

4. After 4 hours, check tails for tenderness.

5. Enjoy with your favorite starch addition rice, potatoes, or pasta.

Chili

Servings: 6
Cooking Time: 120 Minutes

Ingredients:

- 4 lbs of beef chuck roast, trimmed of fat and cut into 1 1/2 inch cubes
- 4 oz bacon, cut into 1/4 inch pieces
- 4 cloves garlic, minced
- 2 jalapeños, cored, seeded, and diced
- 1 large onion, diced
- 4 cups low sodium beef broth
- 2 cups water
- 2 cups dark beer
- 1 cup crushed tomatoes
- 1/4 cup ancho chili powder
- 1/4 cup masa harina
- 2 Tablespoons ground cumin
- 1 Tablespoon chipotle chili powder
- 1 Tablespoon brown sugar
- 2 tsp salt
- 2 tsp dried oregano
- 2 tsp unsweetened cocoa powder
- 1 tsp ground coriander
- 1/4 tsp cinnamon
- Salt and Pepper

Directions:

1. Preheat the grill to 500°F using direct heat with a cast iron grate installed.
2. Place the bacon in the bottom of a cold dutch oven and place the pot in the grill with the dome closed for 10 minutes, or until the bacon is crispy.
3. Remove the bacon from the pot and set aside.
4. Season the beef chunks with salt and pepper and begin browning them in the bacon fat. Work in batches taking care not to crowd the pan. Set aside.
5. Add the spices to the remaining fat and stir for 1 minute until fragrant.
6. Add onion, jalapeño, and garlic to the pan and cook until soft, 5 minutes.
7. Add back bacon and beef and pour in beer, water, and beef broth.
8. Reduce the heat in the grill to 300°F.
9. Cover the dutch oven and lower the dome for 1 hour.
10. Remove the lid of the dutch oven and stir in the masa harina until the chili begins to thicken.
11. Serve with cheese, sour cream, lime wedges, and fresh cilantro.

Smoked Brisket Roll

Servings:10

Cooking Time: 650 Minutes

Ingredients:

- 1 brisket flat, fat cap on, about 6 lbs (2.7 kg)
- 1 cup brisket rub
- ½ bag Jack Daniels wood chips, soaked overnight in water
- Bardough House Slaw
- 10 country loaf rolls
- Salted farm butter for the rolls
- 1½ cups (360 ml) brown sugar
- 1 cup (240 ml) kosher salt
- 1 cup (240 ml) ground espresso beans
- ¼ cup (60 ml) freshly ground black pepper
- ¼ cup (60 ml) garlic powder
- 2 Tbsp (30 ml) ground cinnamon
- 2 Tbsp (30 ml) ground cumin
- 2 Tbsp (30 ml) cayenne pepper
- 1½ cups (150 g) green cabbage, thinly sliced
- 1½ cups (150 g) red cabbage, thinly sliced
- 1¼ cups (150 g) julienned carrots
- 1/3 cup (40 g) dried cranberries
- 2 Tbsp (30 ml) mustard
- 1 cup (240 ml) mayo
- Salt to taste
- 1 lb (455 g) stone ground flour
- 1½ cups (355 g) filtered water
- 2¼ tsp (7 g) fresh yeast
- 5 g salt
- 3 Tbsp + 1 tsp (50 ml) extra virgin olive oil

Directions:

1. Coat the brisket on all sides with an even layer of rub. Let the meat to rest for 1 hour at room temperature or until the rub starts to turn pasty.

2. Preheat the grill to 225°F using direct heat with a cast iron grate installed.

3. Place the brisket, fat side up, on the grill. After 8 hours check meat periodically. Poke the meat in a few places; the fat should separate under your finger. When the brisket reaches an internal temperature of 200°F, remove it from the kamado grill onto a rimmed baking sheet to rest for 30 minutes.

4. Cut the brisket in thin slices against the grain. Cut the rolls in half and butter on both sides. Add sliced brisket and slaw and enjoy!

5. Mix all rub ingredients together and refrigerate.

6. Mix all slaw ingredients together and refrigerate.

7. Dissolve the yeast in half the water. Place the flour and salt in a mixing bowl; add the yeast mixture and the oil.

8. Knead the dough by hand for 10 minutes, slowly adding the rest of the water. Allow to rest for 1 hour or until double in size. Divide into 10 equal size rounds. Shape into balls and allow to rest for an additional hour.

9. Set the kamado grill for indirect cooking with the platesetter and a Pizza and Baking Stone at 400°F. Place the rolls 1 inch (2.5 cm) apart on the preheated stone. Spritz lightly with water and bake for 15 minutes, then remove to a cooling rack.

Grilled Steak And Taylor Farms Caesar Salad

Servings:2

Cooking Time: 16 Minutes

Ingredients:
- 2-inch filet
- Classic Steakhouse Seasoning
- 1 Taylor Farms Caesar Chopped Kit

Directions:
1. Preheat the grill to 400°F using direct heat with a cast iron grate installed.
2. Season the steak on both sides with the Classic Steakhouse Seasoning. Set aside until it reaches room temperature.
3. Place the steak on the grid and grill for 8 minutes per side or until the internal temperature reaches 130°F. Remove the steak from the kamado grill and let rest for 10 minutes, then slice.
4. While the steak is resting, mix the Taylor Farms Caesar Chopped Kit. Place on the steak top of the Caesar salad and serve.

Asian Flank Steak

Servings: 4

Cooking Time: 14 Minutes

Ingredients:
- 1 (1 1/2 –pound) flank steak
- 1 recipe Spicy Thai Marinade

Directions:
1. Pour marinade into a large zip top bag and place steak inside. Refrigerate at least 30 minutes or up to overnight.
2. Remove the meat from the fridge while you preheat the grill to 500°F using direct heat with a cast iron grate installed.
3. Grilling:
4. Place flank steak on the grid and close the dome for 3 minutes.
5. Flip the steak over and cook an additional 2 minutes.
6. Close all of the vents and let the steak sit for 5 minutes or until the internal temperature reaches 130°F.
7. Remove the steak and allow it to rest for 10 minutes before slicing thinly on the bias.

Pitmaster Ribeyes

Servings: 4

Cooking Time: 75 Minutes

Ingredients:

- 4 ribeye steaks
- 1/4 cup spice rub

Directions:

1. Season both sides of all steaks with spice rub and allow to sit for 15 minutes.
2. Grilling:
3. Preheat the grill to 225°F using direct heat with a cast iron grate installed. Add soaked wood chips to the charcoal. (We like pecan or apple.)
4. Place the steaks on the grid and allow to smoke for 1 hour.
5. Remove the steaks from the grill.
6. Heat the grill to 500°F.
7. Place steaks on the grid and close the dome for 3 minutes.
8. Flip the steaks over and cook an additional 2 minutes.
9. Close all of the vents and let the steaks sit for 5 minutes or until the internal temperature reaches 130°F.
10. Allow the steaks to rest for 5-10 minutes before slicing.

Melissa's Hatch Steak Sandwich

Servings:4

Cooking Time: 5 Minutes

Ingredients:

- ½ teaspoon salt
- ½ teaspoon black pepper
- 1 teaspoon Melissa's Hatch Chile Powder
- ½ teaspoon onion powder
- ½ teaspoon garlic powder
- ½ teaspoon dried thyme
- 1 pound beef sirloin, thinly sliced into 2-inch long strips
- 3 tablespoons vegetable oil, divided
- 1 onion, sliced
- 2 Hatch Chiles, roasted, peeled, stemmed, seeded, and halved
- 4 thin slices Swiss cheese
- 4 hoagie rolls, split lengthwise

Directions:

1. In a large bowl, mix together the salt, pepper, Hatch Chile powder, onion powder, garlic powder, and thyme. Add the beef strips and toss to coat. Sprinkle the seasoning mixture over the meat.
2. In a skillet over medium-high heat, heat 11/2 tablespoons of the oil until shimmering. Add the beef, sauté it to desired doneness, and remove it from the pan and set aside. Add the remaining 11/2 tablespoons of oil to the skillet, and sauté the onions and Hatch Chiles until the unions are softened, about 5 minutes.
3. Preheat the oven to broil. Divide the meat among the bottoms of the 4 rolls, layer on the onions and Hatch Chiles, then top with sliced cheese. Set on a baking sheet and broil to melt the cheese. Cover with tops of rolls and serve.

Slow Roasted Leg Of Lamb

Servings:6
Cooking Time: 90 Minutes

Ingredients:

- 1 (5 to 6-pound) leg of lamb
- 5 cloves garlic, thinly sliced
- 20 (1-inch) pieces fresh rosemary
- 1/4 cup extra-virgin olive oil
- 1 teaspoon kosher salt
- 1 teaspoon freshly ground black pepper

Directions:

1. Preheat the grill to 300°F using direct heat with a cast iron grate installed.

2. Using a small paring knife, make 20 (1-inch) cuts evenly all over the lamb.

3. Stuff each hole with a slice of garlic and a piece of rosemary. Brush the lamb with the olive oil and season with salt and pepper.

4. Transfer the lamb to the V-Rack and set the V-Rack in the Drip Pan. Put the Drip Pan on the grid and close the lid of the grill. Roast for 2 to 2 1/2 hours, until the instant read thermometer registers 140ºF/60ºC. Remove the pan from the heat and let cool for 10 minutes.

5. Carve the lamb, transfer to a platter, and serve immediately.

Smoked Strip Loin

Servings: 6
Cooking Time: 120 Minutes

Ingredients:

- 6lb (2.7kg) New York strip loin
- for the zhug
- 8 garlic cloves, peeled
- 5 poblano pepper, left whole
- 1⁄2 cup chopped fresh cilantro
- 2 tbsp lemon juice
- 1 tbsp ground coriander
- 1 tbsp ground cardamom
- 1 tbsp kosher salt
- 1⁄2 cup chopped fresh flat-leaf parsley
- 4 tbsp gochujang paste, divided
- 3⁄4 cup canola oil, plus more as needed
- to smoke
- apple, hickory, or apricot wood chunks

Directions:

1. Preheat the grill to 275°F (135°C). Once hot, add the wood chunks and install the heat deflector and a standard grate. Wrap garlic in aluminum foil, place garlic and poblanos on the grate, close the lid, and cook until beginning to soften and char, about 15 to 20 minutes.

2. To make the zhug, in a food processor, combine garlic, poblanos, cilantro, lemon juice, coriander, cardamom, salt, parsley, and 2 tbsp gochujang. Pulse until a coarse paste forms. Reserve 1⁄4 cup zhug and set aside. Transfer the remaining zhug to an airtight container, stir in oil, and refrigerate until ready to use.

3. In a small bowl, combine reserved 1⁄4 cup zhug and the remaining 2 tbsp gochujang, and add just enough oil to fully combine. Rub loin with the mixture, wrap tightly in plastic wrap, and refrigerate for at least 4 hours or overnight.

4. Remove loin from the fridge and allow to come to room temperature. Place loin on the grate, close the lid, and smoke until the internal temperature reaches 120°F (49°C), about 90 minutes. Remove loin from the grill and place on a baking pan.

5. Slightly close the top and bottom vents to raise the temperature to 500°F (260°C), top loin with half the refrigerated zhug, and place the pan on the grate. Close the lid and cook until the internal temperature reaches 130°F (54°C), about 8 to 10 minutes.

6. Remove loin from the grill and let rest for 20 minutes. Slice and serve with the remaining zhug, adjusting the seasoning as needed.

Holiday Sirloin Roast

Servings: 6
Cooking Time:180 Minutes

Ingredients:

- 1 (5-8 lb) sirloin roast
- 1/4 cup Dijon mustard
- 2 Tablespoons fresh rosemary, chopped
- 1/2 tsp salt
- 1/4 tsp pepper
- 3 cloves garlic, minced

Directions:

1. Bring the roast to room temperature for 30 minutes before cooking.
2. Sprinkle the roast with salt and pepper.
3. Spread liberally with Dijon and press rosemary and garlic into the mustard.
4. Grilling:
5. Preheat the grill to 325°F using direct heat with a cast iron grate installed.
6. Place the roast directly on the grid and close the dome for 2 1/2 to 3 hours or until the internal temperature reaches 130°F.
7. Remove from the grill onto a board and allow it to rest for 20 minutes before carving.

Sloppy Joes

Servings: 4
Cooking Time: 40 Minutes

Ingredients:

- 1 lb ground beef
- 1/4 cup onion, finely chopped
- 1/4 cup bell pepper, finely chopped
- 1 clove garlic, finely chopped
- 1/2 cup tomato sauce
- 1/4 cup ketchup
- 2 Tablespoons brown sugar
- 1 Tablespoon brown mustard
- Salt & Pepper

Directions:

1. Preheat the grill to 400°F using direct heat with a cast iron grate installed with the dutch oven on the grid.
2. Place all ingredients in the dutch oven and stir.
3. Cover the dutch oven and lower the dome for 30-40 minutes or until the beef is cooked through.
4. Serve on hamburger buns.

Steak With Caramelized Onions

Servings:2

Cooking Time: 5 Minutes

Ingredients:

- 1 shoulder steak
- 2 Tablespoons olive oil, separated
- 1 medium white onion, sliced
- 1 cup Miller LITE beer
- 1 tablespoon Plugra unsalted butter
- Salt and pepper, to taste

Directions:

1. Preheat the grill to 450°F using direct heat with a cast iron grate installed. In the meantime, heat a large skillet over medium high heat and add to tablespoons of the oil and swirl to coat well. Add the sliced onions. Sauté the onions until caramelized (about 4 minutes). Add beer and simmer until liquid is reduced by 75%. Add the butter and swirl until melted. Set aside and keep warm.

2. Rub all sides of the steak with one tablespoon of oil and season to taste with the salt and pepper. Place on hot grill and sear for three minutes per side. Lower the heat and continue to cook; turning often until done to your liking. Remove the steaks from the grill and let them rest for 5-8 minutes.

3. Place the steak on serving plates and spoon caramelized onions over the top.

Jim Beam Hamburgers

Servings:2

Cooking Time: 12 Minutes

Ingredients:

- 1 pound ground beef
- 1 (1 oz) package onion soup mix
- 2 tablespoons Worcestershire sauce
- 2 tablespoons Jim Beam bourbon
- Dash hot pepper sauce (recommended: Tabasco)
- Hamburger buns, for serving

Directions:

1. Preheat the grill to 375°F using direct heat with a cast iron grate installed. Using your hands, combine all ingredients in a medium bowl, mixing just to combine. Divide meat into 4 portions and form each into patty using your hands. Grill for 4 to 6 minutes on both sides for medium-rare to medium doneness. If desired, place buns, cut side down on the grill, until toasted, about 1 to 2 minutes. Serve burgers on buns.

Corned Beef And Cabbage

Servings:8

Cooking Time: 30 Minutes

Ingredients:

- 3 pounds corned beef brisket with spice packet
- 1 can or bottle Irish Stout
- 10 small red potatoes
- 5 carrots, peeled and cut into 3-inch pieces
- 1 large head cabbage, cut into large wedges
- 2 bay leaves

Directions:

1. Preheat the grill to 450°F using direct heat with a cast iron grate installed.

2. Place the corned beef in the dutch oven and cover with water and the stout; add the spice packet that came with the corned beef and cover. Place on the cooking grid and bring to a boil, then reduce the temperature to 350°F. Simmer approximately 50 minutes per pound or until tender.

3. After two hours, add whole potatoes and carrots, and cook for 15 minutes. Add cabbage and cook for 15 more minutes. Remove meat and let rest for 15 minutes.

4. Place vegetables in a bowl and cover with some of the broth. Slice meat across the grain and serve with warm bread.

Hoisin Grilled Rabbit

Servings: 8

Cooking Time: 25 Minutes

Ingredients:

- 2 rabbits, about 4lb (1.8kg) in total, quartered
- 1/4 cup hoisin sauce
- for the brine
- 2/3 cup kosher salt
- 2/3 cup packed light brown sugar
- 4 tbsp pickling spice
- 8 cups hot water
- 2 tbsp Chinese five-spice powder
- for the pickled carrots
- 1/4 cup sugar
- 1/2 cup rice vinegar
- 1/2 cup water
- 2 tbsp hot sauce
- 2lb (1kg) carrots, peeled
- for the succotash
- 1 red bell pepper, left whole
- 2 ears of corn, shucked
- 2 tbsp extra virgin olive oil
- 1 cup diced red onion
- 1 large garlic clove, minced
- 1 cup fresh edamame, shelled
- kosher salt and freshly ground black pepper
- 1 tbsp thinly sliced fresh basil

Directions:

1. To make the brine, in a large bowl, whisk together salt, brown sugar, pickling spice, and water until salt and sugar have dissolved. Add ice cubes a few at a time until the liquid is no longer hot. Stir in Chinese five-spice powder. Place rabbit pieces in a large resealable plastic bag and add brine to fully cover. (Any extra brine can be refrigerated and saved for a later use.) Refrigerate for 1 hour.

2. Preheat the grill to 325°F (163°C) using direct heat with a cast iron grate installed. Place carrots, pepper, and corn on the grate, close the lid, and grill until beginning to soften and char, about 6 to 8 minutes. Remove the vegetables from the grill, place a dutch oven on the grate to heat, and close the lid. Once the vegetables are cool enough to handle, cut the kernels from the cobs, seed and dice pepper, and slice carrots into rounds.

3. To make the pickled carrots, in a small saucepan, combine sugar, vinegar, and water. Place on the stovetop over high heat and bring to a boil. Reduce heat to low and stir in the hot sauce. Remove from the heat. Pack the sliced carrots into several airtight containers and pour the hot pickling solution over the carrots to cover. Cover the containers with lids, let cool to room temperature, and refrigerate for at least 2 hours before using. (Pickled carrots can be made in advance and will keep for up to 6 months in the fridge.)

4. Remove rabbit from the brine and pat dry with paper towels. Lightly brush with hoisin sauce and place on the grate next to the dutch oven. To the dutch oven, add oil, onion, garlic, edamame, and grilled pepper and corn. Leave the dutch oven uncovered, close the grill lid, and grill rabbit until the meat reaches an internal temperature of 160°F (71°C) and the onions are soft, about 10 to 15 minutes, turning the rabbit pieces once. Season the succotash with salt and pepper to taste and sprinkle with basil.

5. Remove rabbit and the dutch oven from the grill and serve immediately with the pickled carrots.

DESSERTS

Upside Down Triple Berry Pie

Servings: 8
Cooking Time: 35 Minutes

Ingredients:

- 6 cups frozen triple berry mix
- 2 Tablespoons lemon juice
- 1 refrigerated pie crust
- 1 cup sugar, divided
- 4 Tablespoons cornstarch

Directions:

1. Place a liner in the dutch oven.
2. In a separate bowl, combine frozen berries with 3/4 cup sugar, cornstarch, and lemon juice.
3. Pour berries into the bottom of the lined dutch oven.
4. Unroll pie crust and place on top of berry mixture.
5. Cut 4 vent holes into the crust.
6. Sprinkle remaining sugar over the pie crust.
7. Grilling:
8. Preheat the grill to 425°F using direct heat with a cast iron grate installed.
9. Cover the dutch oven and place on the grid.
10. Lower the dome for 35 minutes or until the crust is golden and the berry mixture has thickened.
11. Cut the crust as you would any pie.
12. Serve a piece of crust topped with ice cream and a scoop of the thickened berry mixture.

Berry Upside-down Cake

Servings: 10

Cooking Time: 30 Minutes

Ingredients:

- 10 tbsp unsalted butter, at room temperature, divided
- 1 cup packed light brown sugar, divided
- 11oz (315g) fresh seasonal berries
- 1 large egg
- 1 tsp pure vanilla extract
- 2⁄3 cup sour cream
- 11⁄3 cups all-purpose flour
- 1 tbsp baking powder
- 1⁄4 tsp baking soda
- 1⁄2 tsp kosher salt
- 1⁄4 tsp ground cinnamon
- fresh mint leaves, to garnish
- whipped cream, to serve

Directions:

1. Preheat the grill to 350°F (177°C) using indirect heat with a standard grate installed and a cast iron skillet on the grate. Melt 2 tbsp butter in the skillet and swirl to coat. Remove the skillet from the grill. Sprinkle 1⁄3 cup brown sugar over butter, pour in berries, and shake the skillet until berries are evenly spread out. Set aside.

2. In the bowl of a stand mixer fitted with the paddle attachment, cream together remaining 8 tbsp butter and 2⁄3 cup brown sugar until fluffy. Add egg, vanilla, and sour cream, and beat to combine.

3. In a medium bowl, sift together flour, baking powder, baking soda, salt, and cinnamon. Gradually add the dry ingredients to the butter and egg mixture until just incorporated. (The batter will be thick.) Using a rubber spatula, scoop the batter into the skillet, smoothing it over berries.

4. Place the skillet on the grate, close the lid, and bake until golden brown and a cake tester inserted into the middle of the cake comes out clean, about 30 minutes. Remove the skillet from the grill and place on a wire rack to cool for 15 minutes.

5. To serve, flip the cake upside down on a large serving platter and release from the skillet, leaving the berries on top. Garnish with fresh mint leaves, and serve with a dollop of whipped cream.

Almond Cream Cake

Servings: 16
Cooking Time: 45 Minutes

Ingredients:

- 2 cups butter, softened
- 3 cups sugar
- 6 cups cake flour
- 1 tsp kosher salt
- 4 tsp baking powder
- 2 cups whole milk
- 2 tsp almond extract
- 10 large eggs, whites only
- sliced almonds, to decorate
- for the frosting
- 1¼ cups all-purpose flour
- 2 cups whole milk
- ½ tsp almond extract
- 1 tbsp vanilla bean paste
- 2 cups butter, softened
- 2 cups sugar

Directions:

1. In the bowl of a stand mixer fitted with the paddle attachment, cream butter until white in appearance. Add sugar and beat until fluffy. In a large bowl, sift together flour, salt, and baking powder. Add the flour mixture to the butter mixture in three stages, alternating with the milk and almond extract and mixing after each addition until just combined.

2. In a large bowl, beat egg whites until they form stiff peaks. Using a spatula, gently fold egg whites into the cake batter, taking care not to overmix.

3. Preheat the grill to 350°F (177°C) using indirect heat with a standard grate installed. Line an11 x18-in (28 x 46cm) grill-safe baking pan with parchment paper and lightly grease with cooking spray. Pour the batter into the pan, place on the grate, close the lid, and bake until the top springs back when touched, about 27 to 30 minutes.

4. Remove the cake from the grill and place on a wire rack to cool for 10 minutes. Use a knife to loosen the edges, and transfer the cake to a wire rack to cool completely.

5. To make the frosting, on the stovetop in a saucepan over medium-low heat, whisk together flour and milk until mixture thickens to the consistency of mashed potatoes, about 12 to 15 minutes. Stir constantly, and lower the heat if needed. Remove the saucepan from the heat and place in a bowl of ice for 5 to 10 minutes to hasten the cooling process and bring the mixture to room temperature. Once cool, stir in almond extract.

6. In the bowl of a stand mixer, cream together vanilla paste, butter, and sugar until the mixture is light and fluffy and sugar is completely dissolved. Add the flour mixture, and beat until it has the appearance of whipped cream, scraping the sides of the bowl as needed.

7. Spread the frosting evenly over the cooled cake and sprinkle sliced almonds over top to decorate before serving.

3 Ingredient Fruit Cobbler

Servings: 8
Cooking Time: 30 Minutes

Ingredients:
- 1 stick butter, sliced
- 2 (29 oz) cans fruit, drained but reserving 1/2 cup of the liquid
- 1 yellow cake mix

Directions:
1. Line the dutch oven with a liner
2. Pour fruit into the bottom of the dutch oven with 1/2 cup of reserved liquid
3. Sprinkle the top with cake mix
4. Dot the top with butter.
5. Grilling:
6. Preheat the grill to 350°F using direct heat with a cast iron grate installed.
7. Cover the dutch oven and place on the grid of the grill.
8. Lower the dome for 30 minutes.
9. Allow the cobbler to sit for 10 minutes off the heat before serving.

Best Banana Bread

Servings: 6
Cooking Time: 40 Minutes

Ingredients:
- 1 cup plain yogurt
- 1/4 cup butter
- 3 very ripe bananas, peeled
- 2 eggs
- 2 cups flour
- 2/3 cups sugar
- 3/4 tsp salt
- 1/2 tsp vanilla extract
- 1/2 tsp baking soda
- 1/4 tsp baking powder

Directions:
1. In a blender, combine bananas, yogurt, sugar, butter, vanilla, and eggs until smooth.
2. In a large bowl, sift together flour, salt, baking powder, and baking soda.
3. Gradually add the wet ingredients into the dry ingredients and gently stir to combine. DO NOT OVER MIX.
4. Line a dutch oven with a liner.
5. Pour batter into the dutch oven and cover.
6. Grilling:
7. Preheat the grill to 350°F using direct heat with a cast iron grate installed and place the dutch oven on the grid.
8. Lower the dome for 30 minutes or until a toothpick inserted into the center comes out clean.

Peach Dutch Baby

Servings: 8
Cooking Time: 25 Minutes

Ingredients:

- 8 oz frozen peaches, thawed (or 3 ripe peaches, peeled and sliced)
- 1 cup whole milk
- 4 eggs
- 1 cup flour
- 1/4 cup sugar
- 1/4 cup butter
- 1 tsp vanilla
- 1 tsp cinnamon
- 1/2 tsp salt

Directions:

1. In a blender, combine milk, flour, sugar, vanilla, cinnamon, salt, and eggs until smooth.
2. Grilling:
3. Preheat the grill to 425°F using direct heat with a cast iron grate installed.
4. Place the dutch oven on the grid of the grill and melt the butter.
5. Line the bottom of the pot with peaches and pour over milk and egg mixture.
6. Close the dome for 20 minutes or until the top of the Dutch Baby is golden brown.
7. Serve with a sprinkling of powdered sugar.

Apple Cake

Servings: 12
Cooking Time: 60 Minutes

Ingredients:

- 2 (21 oz) cans apple pie filling
- 1 (14 oz) jar caramel ice cream topping
- 1 box yellow cake mix, prepared according to package directions and mixed with 2 tsp cinnamon

Directions:

1. Prepare cake according to package directions.
2. Line a dutch oven with a liner.
3. Pour pie filling into the bottom of the dutch oven.
4. Top with caramel ice cream topping.
5. Top with prepared cake mix.
6. Grilling:
7. Preheat the grill to 350°F using direct heat with a cast iron grate installed.
8. Cover the dutch oven and place on the grid of the grill.
9. Lower the dome and cook for 1 hour.
10. Serve warm with whipped cream or ice cream.

Apple Pizza

Servings: 8

Cooking Time: 5 Minutes

Ingredients:

- 1 pizza dough
- 1 cup apple pie filling
- 1/4 cup vanilla cake mix
- 2 Tablespoon melted butter
- Vanilla Ice Cream

Directions:

1. Stretch pizza dough into a 14" round and place on a pizza peel.
2. In a small bowl, combine cake mix and melted butter until it forms a crumbly texture.
3. Spread apple pie filling over pizza dough and top with crumb mixture.
4. Grilling:
5. Bake on a pizza stone in a 500°F grill for 5 minutes.
6. Slice and serve with vanilla frosting.

Seasonal Fruit Cobbler

Servings: 12

Cooking Time: 90 Minutes

Ingredients:

- 2lb (1kg) seasonal fruit, washed, pitted (if needed), and sliced or halved if needed
- 1/2 tsp ground cinnamon
- 2 tsp cornstarch (for juicy fruits; omit for pears or apples)
- 4 tbsp butter, plus more for greasing
- 1/2 cup sugar, plus more for sprinkling
- 3/4 cup self-rising flour
- 3/4 cup whole milk
- whipped cream, to serve

Directions:

1. Preheat the grill to 350°F (177°C) using indirect heat with a standard grate installed. Place the fruit on the grate (or in a cast iron skillet if the fruit might fall through the grate), close the lid, and grill until beginning to soften and char, about 7 to 10 minutes. Remove fruit from the grill and place in a large bowl. Sprinkle cinnamon and cornstarch (if using) over fruit, and add a little sugar (if desired). Gently toss to coat and set aside.

2. Grease a 9-in (23-cm) grill-safe baking pan with butter. On the stovetop in a small saucepan, heat 4 tbsp butter over medium-low heat until beginning to brown, about 10 to 15 minutes.

3. In a medium bowl, whisk together butter, sugar, flour, and milk. Transfer fruit to the prepared baking pan and spread the batter evenly over top. Place the pan on the grate, close the lid, and bake until golden brown and bubbly, about 1 hour. In the last 10 minutes of cooking, sprinkle a light amount of sugar over top. Remove the cobbler from the grill, and serve warm with whipped cream on top.

Lemon Poppy Seed Cake

Servings: 10

Cooking Time: 45 Minutes

Ingredients:

- 1 tsp poppy seeds
- 2 lemons, zested and juiced
- 1 vanilla cake mix prepared according to package directions, substituting melted butter for oil and buttermilk for water
- 1 lb powdered sugar
- 4 ounces cream cheese
- 1 stick butter, softened
- 1/2 tsp vanilla
- 1/2 tsp lemon extract
- The juice and zest of 1 lemon

Directions:

1. Prepare cake mix according to package directions, substituting melted butter for the oil and buttermilk for the water.
2. Add the lemon zest, lemon juice, and poppy seeds.
3. Line the dutch oven with a liner.
4. Pour prepare cake mix into the liner and cover.
5. Grilling:
6. Preheat the grill to 350°F using direct heat with a cast iron grate installed.
7. Place the dutch oven on the grid and lower the dome for 30-40 minutes or until a toothpick inserted into the center comes out clean.
8. Meanwhile, combine glaze ingredients, adding milk to thin out the glaze if necessary.
9. Remove the cake from the grill and set aside to cool for 10 minutes before pouring glaze over the cake.
10. Serve warm.

Triple Berry Crostata

Servings: 8

Cooking Time: 50 Minutes

Ingredients:

- 1 1/2 cups all-purpose flour
- 11 Tablespoons butter, cut into 1/2 inch cubes
- 3 Tablespoons whole milk
- 2 tsp sugar
- 1 large egg yolk
- 2 cups frozen triple berry blend
- 1/4 cup sugar
- 2 Tablespoons cornstarch

Directions:

1. In a food processor, combine flour and butter and pulse until pea-sized cubes of butter can be seen throughout the flour.
2. Add sugar, egg yolk, and milk and pulse until the dough comes together.
3. Form the dough into a circle, cover tightly with plastic wrap, and refrigerate 20 minutes.
4. Roll the dough into a large round and place on a pizza peel covered in cornmeal.
5. In a bowl, combine fruit, sugar, and cornstarch and pile into the center of the dough.
6. Beginning on one side, fold the dough 1/3 of the way over the fruit, repeating until a free-form tart is formed.
7. Grilling:
8. Preheat the grill to 350°F using direct heat with a cast iron grate installed.
9. Slide the crostata onto the pizza stone and close the dome for 40-55 minutes or until the crust is golden brown.
10. Remove the crostata from the grill and allow to cool slightly before slicing and serving.

Nutella And Strawberry Pizza

Servings: 8

Cooking Time: 5 Minutes

Ingredients:

- 1 pizza dough
- 1/2 lb sliced strawberries
- 1/4 cup Nutella

Directions:

1. Stretch the pizza dough into a 14 inch round and place it on a pizza peel.
2. Spread the dough with the Nutella and top with strawberries.
3. Grilling:
4. Slide the pizza onto the prepared stone in a 500°F grill and cook for 5 minutes.
5. Remove from the stone with a pizza peel and slice into 8 pieces.

Buttermilk Biscuits

Servings: 6
Cooking Time: 15 Minutes

Ingredients:
- 3/4 cups buttermilk
- 1/2 cup butter, cut into 1/2 inch cubes
- 3 cups flour
- 1 1/2 tsp baking powder
- 1/2 tsp salt

Directions:
1. In the bowl of a food processor, combine flour, baking powder, salt and butter and pulse until the butter is the size of small peas.
2. With the food processor going, stream in buttermilk until the dough just comes together.
3. Turn out on a floured surface.
4. Pat the dough to 1/2-inch thickness and fold in half.
5. Pat the dough to 1/2-inch thickness and fold in half again.
6. Pat the dough a third time to 1/2-inch thickness.
7. Using a pizza cutter, cut the dough into 12 square biscuits.
8. Place a sheet of parchment in the bottom of the dutch oven.
9. Place biscuits on the bottom of the dutch oven, being careful that they do not touch. (You may have to do this in two batches.)
10. Grilling:
11. Preheat the grill to 425°F using direct heat with a cast iron grate installed.
12. Cover the dutch oven with the lid and place on the grid.
13. Lower the dome for 12-15 minutes.
14. Biscuits are done when they are golden brown. Serve with butter, honey, or jam.

Whole Apples With Caramel Sauce

Servings: 4
Cooking Time: 60 Minutes

Ingredients:
- 4 Jonathan Apples
- 1 cup packed dark brown sugar
- 1/2 cup half and half
- 4 Tablespoons butter
- 1 tsp vanilla extract

Directions:
1. In a medium saucepan, whisk together the brown sugar, butter, and half and half until melted.
2. Continue whisking 5-7 minutes until the caramel begins to thicken.
3. Add vanilla and set aside to cool before storing in a jar in the fridge.
4. Using a melon baller, scoop the core from the apple.
5. Wrap each apple in aluminum foil.
6. Grilling:
7. Preheat the grill to 225°F using direct heat with a cast iron grate installed for 1 hour.
8. Remove apples from the grill, serve topped with caramel sauce.

Death By Chocolate

Servings: 8

Cooking Time: 60 Minutes

Ingredients:

- 1 chocolate cake mix, prepared according to package directions
- 2 cups chocolate chips
- 1 cup brown sugar
- 1 1/2 cups water
- 1/2 cup cocoa powder
- 1 (10 oz) bag miniature marshmallows

Directions:

1. Prepare cake mix according to package instructions.
2. Line the dutch oven with a liner.
3. In a medium bowl, combine water, brown sugar, and cocoa powder.
4. Pour the mixture into the bottom of the dutch oven.
5. Top with miniature marshmallows
6. Pour prepared cake mix on top.
7. Top with chocolate chips.
8. Grilling:
9. Preheat the grill to 350°F using direct heat with a cast iron grate installed.
10. Place the lid on the dutch oven and set on the grid of the grill.
11. Close the dome for 1 hour.
12. Remove the dutch oven from the grill, uncover, and serve warm.

Chocolate Cake

Servings: 12

Cooking Time: 45 Minutes

Ingredients:

- 2 cups all-purpose flour
- 2 cups sugar
- 2/3 cup cocoa powder
- 2 tsp baking soda
- 1 tsp baking powder
- 1 tsp kosher salt
- 2 large eggs, at room temperature
- 1 cup buttermilk, at room temperature
- 1 cup strong black coffee, warm
- 1/2 cup vegetable oil
- 1 tbsp pure vanilla extract
- flaky sea salt, for topping (optional)
- for the caramel sauce
- 3/4 cup sugar
- 4 tbsp water
- 4 tsp light corn syrup
- 1/4 cup heavy cream
- 1 tsp pure vanilla extract
- 1 1/2 tbsp unsalted butter
- for the frosting
- 12 tbsp unsalted butter, at room temperature
- 2 1/2 cups powdered sugar
- 1 tsp pure vanilla extract
- 1 tbsp heavy cream
- kosher salt

Directions:

1. Preheat the grill to 350°F (177°C) using indirect heat with a standard grate installed. Grease a 9-in (23-cm) round metal cake pan with nonstick cooking spray and line with parchment paper. (Instead of a cake pan, you can also use a well-seasoned dutch oven.)

2. In a large bowl or the bowl of a stand mixer, sift together flour, sugar, cocoa powder, baking soda, baking powder, and salt. In a separate medium bowl, whisk together eggs, buttermilk, coffee, vegetable oil, and vanilla extract.

3. Gradually add the liquid ingredients to the dry ingredients, stopping to scrape the sides and bottom of the bowl, until just combined. (The batter will be thin.) Pour the batter into the prepared cake pan or dutch oven. Place on the grate, close the grill lid, and bake until a toothpick inserted in the center comes out almost clean, about 25 to 30 minutes. Let sit for 5 minutes, then turn out onto a wire rack to cool completely. (Use a butter knife to loosen the edges if needed.)

4. To make the caramel sauce, in a small saucepan, combine sugar, water, and corn syrup. Place on the stovetop over medium heat, and simmer until the mixture is deep amber in color, about 10 to 15 minutes. Slowly and carefully, add heavy cream, whisking constantly, then whisk in vanilla, butter, and a pinch of salt.

5. To make the frosting, in the bowl of a stand mixer fitted with the paddle attachment, beat butter on medium speed until light and fluffy, about 2 to 3 minutes. Add sugar, vanilla extract, heavy cream, and a pinch of salt. Beat on low speed until combined, about 1 minute. Increase the speed to medium-high and beat for 6 minutes. Add 1/2 cup caramel sauce and mix until combined.

6. Spread the frosting evenly over top and sides of the cooled cake, and drizzle with caramel sauce. Sprinkle with flaky sea salt (if desired) before serving.

4 Ingredient, No Knead Bread

Servings: 4

Cooking Time: 30 Minutes

Ingredients:

- 3 cups warm water
- 1 1/2 Tablespoons yeast
- 1 1/2 Tablespoons salt
- 6 1/2 cups bread flour

Directions:

1. In a 4-quart ice cream container, mix all ingredients until they come together. DO NOT KNEAD.
2. Cover, but do not seal the container and allow it to sit in a warm, dry place until it doubles in size, about 30 minutes.
3. Seal the container and place in the fridge for 1 hour.
4. Place a sheet of parchment paper in the bottom of the dutch oven.
5. Pinch off 1/4 of the dough and form into a ball.
6. Place the ball on the parchment paper and allow it to rest while the grill heats.
7. Grilling:
8. Preheat the grill to 425°F using direct heat with a cast iron grate installed.
9. Score the top of the dough ball with an "X".
10. Cover the dutch oven and place it on the grid of the grill.
11. Lower the Dome for 30 minutes.
12. Remove the bread from the dutch oven and allow it to cool before slicing.

S'mores Pizza

Servings: 8

Cooking Time: 5 Minutes

Ingredients:

- 1 pizza dough
- 1/2 cup semi-sweet chocolate chips
- 1/2 cup miniature marshmallows
- 1/4 cup slightly crushed graham crackers

Directions:

1. Stretch dough to a 14" round and place on a pizza peel.
2. Sprinkle dough with chocolate chips, miniature marshmallows, and graham cracker crumbs.
3. Grilling:
4. Slide the pizza onto the prepared stone at 500°F.
5. Cook for 5 minutes, remove from the stone, slice, and serve.

Brownies

Servings: 6
Cooking Time: 30 Minutes

Ingredients:

- 1 1/2 cups flour
- 1 cup white sugar
- 1 cup brown sugar
- 3/4 cups cocoa powder
- 1/2 cup butter, melted
- 1/4 cup vegetable oil
- 2 tsp vanilla
- 1 tsp baking powder
- 1/2 tsp salt
- 4 eggs
- 1/2 cup chocolate chips
- 1/2 chip marshmallows

Directions:

1. In a large bowl, combine butter, oil and sugars.
2. Add eggs, one at a time, stirring in between.
3. Add vanilla and stir.
4. Sift together cocoa powder, baking powder, and flour.
5. Add to the butter and egg mixture and stir until just combined.
6. Grilling:
7. Preheat the grill to 350°F using direct heat with a cast iron grate installed.
8. Line the dutch oven with a liner.
9. Pour the batter into the liner.
10. Cover the dutch oven, place on the grid, and lower the dome for 25-30 minutes or until a toothpick inserted into the middle comes out clean.
11. Remove the lid, top the brownies with chocolate chips and marshmallows and replace the lid for 5 minutes until the toppings are melted.

Grilled Pineapple Sundaes

Servings: 4
Cooking Time: 5 Minutes

Ingredients:

- 4 fresh pineapple spears
- Vanilla Ice Cream
- Jarred Caramel Sauce
- Toasted Coconut

Directions:

1. Place pineapple spears on a 400°F grill and close the dome for 2 minutes.
2. Turn the pineapple and close the dome for another 2 minutes.
3. Turn the pineapple once more and close the dome for another minute.
4. Assembly:
5. Serve pineapple topped with ice cream, caramel sauce, and toasted coconut.

Grilled Plums With Honey And Ricotta

Servings: 4

Cooking Time: 5 Minutes

Ingredients:

- 4 plums, cut in half and pitted
- 1/2 cup whole milk ricotta cheese
- 2 Tablespoons honey
- 1/4 tsp cracked black pepper

Directions:

1. Place the plums, cut side down on a 400°F grill.
2. Close the dome for 5 minutes.
3. Assembly:
4. Serve the plums, cut side up, with a dollop of ricotta, a drizzle of honey, and a sprinkling of cracked black pepper.

Peaches And Pound Cake

Servings: 6

Cooking Time: 5 Minutes

Ingredients:

- 1/2 cup heavy whipping cream
- 2 Tablespoons sour cream
- 3 peaches, halved and pitted
- 1 store-bought pound cake, cut into 6 slices

Directions:

1. Place the peaches, cut side down, on a 400°F grill.
2. Place the pound cake slices alongside the peaches and close the dome for 2 minutes.
3. Flip the pound cake, and close the dome for an additional 2-3 minutes.
4. Assembly:
5. In a stand mixer, whip the whipping cream until stiff peaks form. Fold in the sour cream to combine.
6. Place a slice of pound cake on a plate, top with a peach half, and a dollop of the cream.

Grilled Sopapillas

Servings: 6
Cooking Time: 18 Minutes

Ingredients:

- 1 pizza dough, divided into 6 pieces
- 3 Tablespoons melted butter
- 1/4 cup sugar
- 1 Tablespoon cinnamon

Directions:

1. Stretch dough into round shape.
2. Place the dough directly on the pizza stone in a 500°F grill.
3. Brush with melted butter and top with cinnamon sugar.
4. Close the dome for 3 minutes, then remove.
5. Repeat with remaining dough.

Fresh Peach Crisp

Servings: 4
Cooking Time: 5 Minutes

Ingredients:

- 2 peaches, halved with pits removed
- Vanilla Ice Cream
- 1 cup good quality granola

Directions:

1. Grilling:
2. Place the peach halves, cut side down, on a 400°F grill and cover with the dome for 5 minutes.
3. Assembly:
4. Remove the peaches and place them, cut side up, in a bowl. Top with vanilla ice cream and granola.

Grilled Watermelon With Honey Yogurt

Servings: 4
Cooking Time: 4 Minutes

Ingredients:

- 1 round of watermelon, 1 inch thick
- 1/2 cup Greek-style yogurt
- 1 Tablespoon honey
- 1/4 tsp vanilla

Directions:

1. Place the watermelon on a 400°F grill with the dome down for 1 minute.
2. Turn the watermelon and lower the dome for an additional minute.
3. Assembly:
4. Cut the watermelon in quarters and place each on a small plate.
5. In a small bowl, combine yogurt, honey, and vanilla and spoon equal amounts over the watermelon.
Serve.

PORK

Slow Roasted Pork Belly

Servings:4

Cooking Time: 120 Minutes

Ingredients:

- 2 lbs. pork belly
- Kosher salt
- Your favorite herb rub (Rusty uses Pine Street Market Summer Spice)

Directions:

1. Preheat the grill to 225°F using direct heat with a cast iron grate installed.

2. Place the pork belly fat side up on the grill. Cook for 2 hours or until the internal temperature reaches 165°F.

3. Remove from the kamado grill and let rest for 10 minutes. Slice and serve. If you prefer crisper pork belly, sear the cooked pork belly in a cast iron skillet until crisp.

Pulled Pork Sandwiches

Servings:12

Cooking Time: 480 Minutes

Ingredients:

- One 7 to 8 pound pork butt, fat cap trimmed off
- 2 tablespoons vegetable oil
- Big Time BBQ Rub
- ½ cup apple juice
- 2 cups Dr. BBQ's Carolina Barbecue sauce
- 12 hamburger buns
- ½ cup salt
- ½ cup turbinado sugar
- ¼ cup granulated brown sugar
- 1 tablespoon granulated garlic
- 1 tablespoon granulated onion
- 2 tablespoons paprika
- 2 tablespoon chili powder
- 2 tablespoon freshly ground black pepper
- 2 teaspoons cayenne
- 1 tablespoon thyme leaves
- 1 tablespoon ground cumin
- 1 teaspoon ground nutmeg
- 1 c vinegar
- 2/3 cup catsup
- 2 teaspoons sugar
- 1 teaspoon salt
- 1 teaspoon Worcestershire
- ½ teaspoon red pepper flakes

Directions:

1. Rub the meat with the oil and then sprinkle liberally with the rub. Put in the refrigerator for at least a half hour and up to 12 hours.

2. Preheat the grill to 275°F using direct heat with a cast iron grate installed. Put the butt in the kamado grill and cook until the internal temperature is 160°F; this should take 6 to 8 hours. Lay out a big double piece of heavy duty aluminum foil and put the pork butt in the middle. As you begin to close up the package pour the apple juice over the top of the butt and then seal the package, taking care not to puncture it put it back in the kamado grill and cook until the meat reaches an internal temperature of 195°F; this should take another 2 to 3 hours.

3. Remove the package from the kamado grill to a baking sheet. Open the top of the foil to let the steam out and let it rest for ½ hour. Using heavy neoprene gloves or a pair of tongs and a fork transfer the meat to a big pan. It will be very tender and hard to handle. Discard the juices as they will be quite fatty. Shred the meat, discarding the fat and bones; it should just fall apart. Continue to pull the meat until it's shredded enough to make a sandwich. Add 1 cup of the sauce and mix well. Reserve the additional sauce for serving on the side. Serve on fluffy white buns topped with cole slaw.

4. Combine all ingredients, mix well, and store in an airtight container.

5. In a small saucepan mix together the vinegar, catsup, sugar, salt, Worcestershire and pepper flakes. Cook over low heat for 5 minutes stirring to blend.

Grilled Tequila Chicken

Servings: 12

Cooking Time: 65 Minutes

Ingredients:

- 12 skinless, boneless chicken thighs, about 3lb (1.4kg) in total
- for the marinade
- juice of 4 limes
- 1/4 cup olive oil
- 1 cup tequila
- 2 tsp kosher salt
- 5 garlic cloves
- 1 jalapeño pepper, sliced
- 1/2 bunch of fresh cilantro, chopped
- for the salad
- 1 cup dried black beans
- 1/4 cup tequila
- 2 cups vegetable stock
- 2 Roma tomatoes, diced
- 1/4 cup diced orange bell pepper
- 1/4 cup diced yellow onion
- 1/4 cup diced scallions
- 1/4 cup diced mango
- 1 tbsp chopped fresh cilantro
- 1 jalapeño pepper, seeded and minced
- 4 tbsp sherry vinegar
- juice of 1 lime
- 3 tbsp honey
- 1 tbsp kosher salt
- 1 tsp ground black pepper
- pinch of ground cumin
- 4 ears of corn, shucked

Directions:

1. To make the marinade, add all the marinade ingredients to a food processor and pulse until well combined. Place chicken thighs in a large resealable plastic bag and pour in the marinade mixture. Refrigerate for at least 2 hours or overnight.

2. Place black beans in a medium bowl and add tequila to cover. Cover with plastic wrap and refrigerate overnight. Drain beans and place in a saucepan on the stovetop. Add vegetable stock to cover by 1 inch (5cm) and bring to a boil. Reduce heat to a simmer, cover, and cook until beans are tender but not falling apart, about 30 to 45 minutes.

3. Drain beans and place in a large bowl. Add tomatoes, pepper, onion, scallions, mango, cilantro, jalapeño, vinegar, lime juice, honey, salt, pepper, and cumin. Stir gently until all ingredients are well mixed. Cover and refrigerate for at least 1 hour to allow the flavors to meld.

4. Preheat the grill to 425°F (218°C) using direct heat with a cast iron grate installed. Place corn on the grate and grill until lightly charred, about 6 to 8 minutes. Transfer the corn to a cutting board and cut the kernels from the cobs. Stir kernels into the black bean salad and set aside.

5. Remove chicken thighs from the marinade and place on the grate (discarding the marinade). Close the lid and grill until the internal temperature reaches 165°F (74°C), about 4 to 5 minutes per side, turning only once. Remove thighs from the grill, slice, and serve over the corn and black bean salad.

Smoked Brat Kabobs

Servings:4

Cooking Time: 20 Minutes

Ingredients:

- ½ cup soy sauce
- ¼ cup frozen apple juice concentrate, thawed
- 3 tablespoons hot mustard
- 1 package (14 ounces) Johnsonville Smoked Brats
- 2 medium sweet red peppers, cut into 1 inch pieces
- 1 medium green pepper, cut into 1 inch pieces
- 1 medium yellow summer squash, cut into ½ inch pieces
- 1 medium onion, cut into wedges

Directions:

1. In a resealable plastic bag or bowl, combine soy sauce, apple juice concentrate and hot mustard for marinade. Add vegetables. Seal bag or cover container; refrigerate for one hour.
2. Drain and reserve marinade.
3. Preheat the grill to 350°F using direct heat with a cast iron grate installed.
4. Thread sausage and vegetables alternatively on Flexible Skewers. Brush with reserved marinade.
5. Grill on kamado grill for 15 to 20 minutes or until sausage is hot and vegetables are crisp-tender, turning and basting frequently with reserved marinade.
6. Serve immediately.

Ham & Cheese Panini

Servings:4

Cooking Time: 10 Minutes

Ingredients:

- 8 slices Natures Own 100% whole wheat bread
- ¼ cup spicy brown mustard
- 8 slices sharp white Cheddar cheese
- 2 cups packed baby arugula
- 1 ripe Bartlett pear, cut into 20 thin slices
- ½ pound deli-sliced smoked ham
- Olive Oil

Directions:

1. Preheat the grill to 400°F using direct heat with a cast iron grate installed.
2. Spread mustard evenly over 1 side of each bread slice. Top each of 4 bread slices with 1 slice cheese and half the arugula. Add the pear and ham slices; top with remaining arugula, cheese and bread slices.
3. Press sandwiches together slightly, brush outside of sandwiches lightly with oil Cook sandwiches on the griddle, turning once, until browned and cheese melts.

Double Smoked Maple Bourbon Glazed Ham

Servings:4

Cooking Time: 180 Minutes

Ingredients:

- 1 bone-in half spiral ham
- 3 cups apple juice
- 1 yellow onion, chopped
- 2 tbsp yellow mustard
- BBQ rub
- 1/2 cup pineapple juice
- 1/2 cup maple syrup
- 1 cup bourbon
- 1/4 tsp Dijon mustard
- 1 tsp cinnamon
- 1 cup brown sugar

Directions:

1. Preheat the grill to 275°F using direct heat with a cast iron grate installed.

2. Cover the ham in yellow mustard and add the BBQ rub. Put the apple juice and onion in a roasting pan then place the ham in a roasting rack in the roasting pan. Cook uncovered for 2 hours. Cover with foil and cook another hour. Uncover the ham, glaze, and cook for 30 minutes until the ham reaches an internal temperature of 140°.

3. Remove the ham from the kamado grill and let rest for 10 minutes. Slice and serve.

4. Add glaze ingredients to pan, bring to a boil, and reduce. Cook for 30 minutes or to your desired thickness.

Pork Cacciatore

Servings:4

Cooking Time: 122 Minutes

Ingredients:

- 6 pounds boneless pork shoulder
- 1 1⁄4 teaspoon sea salt
- 3⁄4 teaspoon freshly ground pepper
- 2 tablespoons olive oil
- 1 large red bell pepper, sliced
- 1 large green bell pepper, sliced
- 2 yellow onions, sliced
- 3-4 cloves garlic, chopped
- 2 teaspoons dried basil
- 2 teaspoons dried parsley
- 1 teaspoon dried thyme
- 1 teaspoon red pepper flakes, optional
- 1 cup low sodium chicken broth
- 1 28 ounce can petite diced tomatoes
- 3 tablespoons tomato paste

Directions:

1. Preheat the grill to 350°F using direct heat with a cast iron grate installed.

2. Take pork shoulder out of package and wipe down with a paper towel. Season with salt and pepper.

3. Heat your dutch oven in the grill. Add in oil and let it get nice and hot. Add in pork and sear all sides for about 2 minutes; you want to create a nice sear. Add in peppers, onions and garlic. Cook for about 5 minutes stirring around using a wooden spoon.

4. Add in basil, parsley, thyme and red pepper flakes. Pour in chicken broth and diced tomatoes. Stir to incorporate all of the ingredients. Add in tomato paste and press against the pan with the back of your spoon to help incorporate into the liquid. Cover and let cook 2 hours.

5. Remove from grill. Use a large spoon and skim off the fat then go ahead and pull apart the pork or serve in large chunks with the peppers and onions. Enjoy!

Baby Back Ribs With Apple-bourbon Barbecue Sauce

Servings:6

Cooking Time: 180 Minutes

Ingredients:

- ¼ cup (packed) golden brown sugar
- 3 tablespoons paprika
- 2 teaspoons freshly ground black pepper
- 1 teaspoon ground cumin
- ¼ teaspoon cayenne pepper
- 3 (2 ½ pound) racks pork baby back ribs
- 2 tablespoons (about) kosher salt
- ¾ cup apple cider vinegar
- Apple-Bourbon Barbecue Sauce, warm
- 3 cups hickory wood chips, soaked in water for at least 1 hour
- 2 tablespoons unsalted butter
- 1 onion, chopped
- 2 garlic cloves, finely chopped
- 1 teaspoon paprika
- ½ teaspoon dry mustard
- ½ cup bourbon
- 1 cup apple cider vinegar
- 2 cups chicken broth
- 2 cups ketchup
- ¾ cup packed golden brown sugar
- 2 to 4 canned chipotle chilies in adobo sauce, chopped*
- 2 tablespoons Worcestershire sauce
- 1 teaspoon kosher salt
- ½ teaspoon freshly ground black pepper
- 2 Granny Smith apples, peeled, cored and finely chopped
- 1 lemon, cut in half

Directions:

1. In medium bowl, mix the brown sugar, paprika, black pepper, cumin, and cayenne pepper. Place the ribs on a large baking sheet and rub the ribs with some salt. Sprinkle the spice mixture over the ribs and massage the spices into the meat. Cover and refrigerate for at least 12 hours and up to 24 hours.

2. Preheat the grill to 300°F using direct heat with a cast iron grate installed. Sprinkle 1 cup of the drained wood chips over the coal. Place a foil pan half-filled with water on the platesetter.

3. Combine the vinegar and ¾ cup water in a spray bottle. Season the ribs with salt. Place the ribs on the cooking grate over the water-filled pan. (Don't worry if the ribs extend over the pan, as the pan will still catch the majority of the dripping juices.) Cook, with the dome closed, turning the ribs over and spraying them every 45 minutes or so with the cider mixture, adding another cup of drained wood chips at the same intervals, for about 3 hours, or until the meat is just tender. Do not add more wood chips after the 1 ½ hour point, as too much smoke will give the ribs a bitter flavor.

4. Once the ribs are tender, begin brushing them lightly with the barbecue sauce every few minutes or so, allowing the sauce to set before applying the next coat. Continue brushing the ribs with the sauce, turning occasionally, for about 30 minutes, or until the meat has shrunk from the ends of the bones. Transfer the ribs to a carving board and let rest for about 5 minutes.

5.   To serve: Using a large sharp knife cut the racks into individual ribs. Transfer to a large bowl and toss with enough of the remaining warm barbecue sauce to coat. Arrange the ribs on a platter and serve with the remaining sauce on the side.

6.   In a large saucepan, melt the butter over medium heat. Add the onion and sauté until tender, about 5 minutes. Add the garlic and sauté until very tender, about 3 minutes; stir in the paprika and mustard powder.

7.   Stir in the bourbon then the vinegar and simmer for 3 minutes. Stir in the broth, ketchup, brown sugar, chipotle chilies, Worcestershire sauce, salt and black pepper. Add the apples and squeeze the juice from the lemon into the sauce.

8.   Bring the sauce to a simmer over high heat then reduce the heat to medium-low and simmer, uncovered, until the sauce reduces and thickens slightly, stirring.

Pork Belly & Rice Grits

Servings: 8
Cooking Time: 270 Minutes

Ingredients:

- 3 tbsp vegetable oil
- 2lb pork belly, about 1 in (2.5-cm) thick, cut into 8 pieces
- kosher salt and freshly ground black pepper
- 1 small red onion, roughly chopped
- 2 small carrots, roughly chopped
- 1 bay leaf
- 1/2 tsp coriander seeds
- 4 cups chicken stock, divided
- 1/4 cup rice flour
- 1/2 cup rice grits or hominy grits
- 1/2 cup heavy cream
- 1 cup shredded sharp Cheddar cheese or Fontina (optional)
- 1/2 cup finely chopped kimchi
- for the pickles
- 1/2 tsp sugar
- 1/4 cup unseasoned rice vinegar
- 1/2 cup thinly sliced radishes
- 1/2 red onion
- 2 scallions, thinly sliced on the bias
- to smoke
- oak, apricot, or bourbon barrel wood chunks

Directions:

1. Preheat the grill to 300°F (149°C). Once hot, add the wood chunks and install the heat deflector along with a standard grate and dutch oven. To the hot dutch oven, heat oil until shimmering. Add pork pieces, and season with salt and pepper to taste. Close the grill lid and smoke until pork has browned on all sides, about 10 to 15 minutes. Add onion, carrots, bay leaf, and coriander seeds, close the grill lid, and cook for 5 minutes more.

2. Add 2 cups chicken stock, close the grill lid, and cook until the meat is very tender, about 3 hours. Leave the lid off the dutch oven for the first hour and cover for the remaining cooking time. Transfer cooked pork to a cutting board and let cool slightly. Cut each piece in half crosswise, lightly coat with rice flour, and set aside. Discard the vegetables and reserve the braising liquid.

3. Rinse the dutch oven and return it to the grill. Open the top and bottom vents to raise the grill temperature to 350°F (177°C). Once hot, arrange the floured pork pieces on the grate around the dutch oven (not inside). Roast until the fat has rendered and pork is slightly crispy, about 15 to 20 minutes.

4. Place grits in the dutch oven and toast until just shiny, about 3 minutes. Slowly add cream and the remaining 2 cups stock in three different stages and cook until creamy and tender, about 10 to 15 minutes, stirring every 3 minutes to break up any lumps. Add cheese (if using), and season with salt and pepper to taste.

5. To make the pickles, in a large shallow bowl, whisk together sugar and vinegar until sugar dissolves. Add onions, scallions, and radishes, cover with plastic wrap, and refrigerate for 15 minutes.

6. On the stovetop in a medium saucepan, bring the reserved braising liquid to a boil. Simmer until the volume has decreased by half, about 15 to 20 minutes.

7. Transfer pork and grits to serving dishes. Stir the reduced braising liquid into the grits or as much for the desired consistency, and season with salt and pepper to taste. Serve immediately with kimchi and pickled onions, scallions, and radishes.

Dutch Oven Pork Roast

Servings: 6

Cooking Time: 75 Minutes

Ingredients:

- 1 3-4 lb boneless pork loin roast
- 2 lbs small potatoes (we like reds or Yukon golds)
- 1 lb parsnips, peeled and cut into 1 inch chunks
- 1 Tablespoon fresh thyme
- Salt and Pepper
- 1/4 cup brown mustard
- 2 Tablespoons Worcestershire sauce
- 2 Tablespoons olive oil

Directions:

1. In a cold dutch oven, toss vegetables with olive oil and a sprinkling of salt and pepper.
2. In a small bowl, combine mustard, Worcestershire, and thyme. Paint all over the loin roast.
3. Place the roast on top of the vegetables.
4. Grilling:
5. Preheat the grill to 425°F using direct heat with a cast iron grate installed.
6. Cover the dutch oven and place on the waiting grill.
7. Lower the dome for 1 hour to 1 hour and 15 minutes or until the internal temperature of the roast reaches 155°F
8. Remove the dutch oven from the grill, remove the pork and set aside to rest for 20 minutes before carving. Recover the dutch oven to keep the vegetables warm in the meantime.
9. Serve warm.

Barbecue Pork Shoulder

Servings: 4

Cooking Time: 840 Minutes

Ingredients:

- 1 (6-8 lb) pork shoulder
- 2 cups East Carolina Barbecue Sauce
- 1 cup Basic BBQ Rub
- 2 cups wood chips, soaked in water for a minimum of 1 hour (any wood is great for this recipe)

Directions:

1. Score the skin of pork shoulder with a knife, cutting only through the skin, not the meat.

2. Liberally sprinkle the pork with BBQ Rub, cover tightly in an aluminum pan and refrigerate 4 hours or up to overnight.

3. Remove the pork shoulder from the refrigerator 1 hour before cooking.

4. Grilling:

5. Preheat the grill to 225°F using direct heat with a cast iron grate installed. Add the drained wood chips to the coals and place the plate setter and grid inside the grill.

6. Place the pork shoulder on the grid and close the dome.

7. The grill will hold its heat at this temperature for up to 18 hours, so you can literally set it and forget it.

8. After 12 hours, check the internal temperature of the roast. It will be a deep mahogany color, but if the temperature has been maintained, it will not be burned or dried out. When the internal temperature reaches 200°F, carefully remove the roast with two forks.

9. Gently pull the meat apart and sprinkle with East Carolina Barbecue Sauce. Serve with additional sauce.

Bbq Chicken Quarters

Servings: 4

Cooking Time: 45

Ingredients:

- 4 skin-on, bone-in chicken leg quarters
- for the brine
- 1⁄2 cup kosher salt
- 1⁄2 cup packed light brown sugar
- 3 tbsp pickling spice
- 6 cups hot water
- for the sauce
- 1⁄4 cup molasses
- 2 cups ketchup
- 3 tsp Worcestershire sauce
- 2 tbsp lemon juice
- 1⁄2 tsp Tabasco sauce
- 3⁄8 cup packed dark brown sugar
- 1⁄2 tsp ground cayenne pepper
- 2 garlic cloves, finely minced
- 1 tbsp ground black pepper
- for the rub
- 4 tbsp kosher salt
- 4 tbsp ground black pepper
- 2 tbsp ancho powder

Directions:

1. To make the brine, in a medium bowl, whisk together salt, brown sugar, pickling spice, and water until salt and sugar have dissolved. Add ice cubes a few at a time until the liquid is no longer hot. Place chicken in a resealable plastic bag and add brine to cover. (Any extra brine can be refrigerated and saved for a later use.) Refrigerate for 1 hour.

2. To make the BBQ sauce, in a small saucepan, combine all the sauce ingredients. Place the saucepan on the stovetop over medium heat and simmer for 15 minutes, stirring occasionally. Remove from the heat and set aside.

3. To make the rub, in a small bowl, combine salt, pepper, and ancho powder. Remove chicken from the brine, pat dry with paper towels, and season with some of the rub mixture. Let chicken come to room temperature.

4. Preheat the grill to 425°F (218°C) using indirect heat with a cast iron grate installed. Brush chicken with the BBQ sauce and place on the grate. Close the lid and grill until the internal temperature reaches 170°F (77°C), 20 to 30 minutes, turning to evenly crisp the skin. Brush chicken with the BBQ sauce every 10 minutes while cooking.

5. Remove chicken from the grill and season with more rub mixture to taste. Let rest for 10 minutes. Serve with the remaining BBQ sauce.

Mediterranean Stuffed Chicken

Servings: 4

Cooking Time: 30 Minutes

Ingredients:

- 4 boneless, skinless chicken breasts, about 1½lb (680g) in total
- 3 tbsp extra virgin olive oil
- 2 tbsp kosher salt, plus more as needed
- 2 tbsp ground black pepper, plus more as needed
- 1 tbsp dried marjoram
- for the brine
- ¼ cup kosher salt
- ¼ cup packed light brown sugar
- 2 tbsp pickling spice
- 3 cups hot water
- for the filling
- 8 sun-dried tomatoes in olive oil, drained and minced
- 4 basil leaves, stacked, rolled, and cut crosswise into thin strips
- 4oz (110g) goat cheese, crumbled
- kosher salt and freshly ground black pepper
- to smoke
- apricot, pecan, or wine barrel wood chunks

Directions:

1. To make the brine, in a medium bowl, whisk together salt, brown sugar, pickling spice, and hot water until salt and sugar have dissolved. Add ice cubes a few at a time until the liquid is no longer hot. Place chicken in a large resealable plastic bag and add brine to cover. (Any extra brine can be refrigerated and saved for a later use.) Refrigerate for 30 minutes.

2. To make the filling, in a medium bowl, combine tomatoes, basil, and cheese, and season with salt and pepper to taste.

3. Remove chicken from the brine, pat dry with paper towels, and cut a slit in the side of each chicken breast to create a pocket. Fill the cavities with equal amounts of filling and close up the pockets with toothpicks soaked in water. Lightly coat the breasts with olive oil, and sprinkle with salt, pepper, and marjoram.

4. Preheat the grill to 325°F (163°C). Once hot, add the wood chunks and install the heat deflector and a standard grate. Place chicken on the grate, close the lid, and smoke until chicken reaches an internal temperature of 165°F (74°C), about 20 to 30 minutes.

5. Remove chicken from the grill and serve immediately.

Grilled Chicken Breasts

Servings: 4

Cooking Time: 15 Minutes

Ingredients:

- 4 skinless, boneless chicken breasts, about 11⁄2lb (680g) in total
- kosher salt and freshly ground black pepper
- 2 nectarines, halved and pitted
- 1 jalapeño pepper, seeded and minced
- 2 cups blackberries, roughly chopped
- 4 tbsp chopped fresh cilantro
- 2 tbsp balsamic vinegar, plus more to taste
- for the brine
- 1⁄4 cup kosher salt
- 1⁄4 cup packed light brown sugar
- 2 tbsp pickling spice
- 3 cups hot water

Directions:

1. To make the brine, in a medium bowl, whisk together all the brine ingredients until salt and sugar have dissolved. Add ice cubes a few at a time until the liquid is no longer hot. Place chicken in a resealable plastic bag and add the brine to cover. (Any extra brine can be refrigerated and saved for a later use.) Refrigerate for 30 minutes.

2. Remove chicken from the brine, pat dry with paper towels, and season with salt and pepper to taste. Set aside and allow to come to room temperature.

3. Preheat the grill to 350°F (177°C) using direct heat with a cast iron grate installed. Place nectarines on the grate skin side up, close the lid, and grill until softened and slightly charred, about 2 minutes. Remove from the grill and dice.

4. In a medium bowl, combine nectarines, jalapeño, blackberries, and cilantro. Add vinegar and toss to combine, adding more vinegar (if desired).

5. Spoon some of the liquid from the salsa over the chicken breasts and rub into the meat. Place chicken on the grate, close the lid, and grill until the meat reaches an internal temperature of 160°F (71°C), about 4 to 6 minutes per side. Remove chicken from the grill and top with the blackberry salsa before serving.

Wild Boar Ribs

Servings:10

Cooking Time: 100 Minutes

Ingredients:

- 6 lbs. wild boar ribs, cut into 1 rib pieces
- ¾ cup soy sauce
- ⅔ cup dry sherry
- ½ cup packed dark brown sugar
- 6 cloves garlic, minced
- 1 Tbs. cayenne pepper
- 1 Tbs. grated fresh ginger
- 2 tsp. Chinese five-spice powder

Directions:

1. Trim excess fat from ribs. In 13 X 9 Drip Pan, arrange ribs in single layer.

2. For marinade, combine remaining ingredients in medium saucepan. Cook over medium heat until sugar is dissolved. Remove from heat; cool slightly. Pour marinade over ribs. Cover and refrigerate 1 hour, turning ribs once. Cover Drip Pan with foil.

3. Preheat the grill to 300°F using direct heat with a cast iron grate installed.

4. Place Drip Pan on cooking grid and cook for 45 minutes.

5. Remove ribs from Drip Pan and place on cooking grid. Cook 45 to 60 minutes longer or until ribs are tender, turning and brushing with marinade occasionally. Brush ribs again with marinade just before serving.

Mona Lisa's Glazed Smoked Ham

Servings:4

Cooking Time: 270 Minutes

Ingredients:

- 1 Ham 10-12 lbs
- 1-20 oz. can round sliced pineapple
- 1 jar maraschino cherries
- 2 boxes brown sugar

Directions:

1. Preheat the grill to 350°F using direct heat with a cast iron grate installed..

2. Rinse ham with cold water, pat dry, and set aside.

3. Take the juice from the pineapple and mix well with the brown sugar to make a nice thick syrupy glaze. Next add the pineapple to the ham putting a cherry in the hole of each pineapple round. Finally pour the glaze over the ham.

4. Loosely cover the ham with aluminum foil and cook for 3-4 hours basting the ham with the pan juice every 30 min.

5. Let stand for 30 min. Slice and serve.

Pork Curry

Servings: 6

Cooking Time: 20 Minutes

Ingredients:

- 2 pork tenderloins, about 3lb (1.4kg) in total, trimmed, silverskin removed, and cut into 2-in (.5-cm) pieces
- 3 cups cooked white rice
- naan bread, to serve (optional)
- for the marinade
- 4 dried red chile peppers
- 1/3 cup white vinegar
- 2 tsp ground cumin
- 1 tsp ground black pepper
- 1/2 tsp cinnamon
- 3 tsp ground cardamom
- 1 tsp ground cloves
- pinch of ground nutmeg
- 1 tsp grated fresh ginger
- 5 garlic cloves, peeled
- 1/2 cup olive oil
- 2 medium yellow onions, roughly chopped
- 1 tsp sugar
- kosher salt
- for the pickled mango
- 1/2 cup apple cider vinegar
- 1 tbsp sugar
- 1/2 tsp kosher salt
- 1 cup hot water
- 1 tbsp Vindaloo curry seasoning
- 1 ripe mango, peeled and sliced

Directions:

1. To make the marinade, in a small bowl, cover peppers with vinegar and let soak for 10 minutes. Transfer peppers and vinegar to a food processor, add remaining marinade ingredients, and blend until smooth. Transfer half the marinade to a resealable plastic bag. Reserve the remaining marinade and set aside.

2. Place pork pieces in the bag with the marinade and squeeze out any excess air. Refrigerate for at least 2 hours and up to 24 hours. Before grilling, remove from the fridge and bring to room temperature.

3. To make the pickled mango, in a small bowl, whisk together vinegar, sugar, and salt until sugar and salt have dissolved. Pack mango in a small jar and pour the vinegar mixture over top to cover. Let sit at room temperature for 1 hour.

4. Preheat the grill to 425°F (218°C) using direct heat with a cast iron grate installed and a dutch oven on the grate. Remove pork pieces from the marinade and place on the grate around the dutch oven (not inside). Close the grill lid and grill until the internal temperature reaches 140°F (60°C), about 8 to 12 minutes.

5. Transfer the grilled pork pieces to the dutch oven and add the cooked rice, reserved marinade, and pickled mango. (Discard pickling liquid or refrigerate in a sealable container for future use.) Cook until warmed through, about 5 to 7 minutes, stir occasionally. Serve immediately with warm naan (if desired).

Swineapple

Servings:2
Cooking Time: 90 Minutes

Ingredients:

- 1 pineapple, whole
- 1lb pork tenderloin
- ½ pack bacon
- Pork Rub
- Dizzy Pig Pineapple Head Seasoning

Directions:

1. Preheat the grill to 240°F using direct heat with a cast iron grate installed. Cut the pork tenderloin to about the size of your pineapple. Rub the tenderloin with your favorite pork rub. Cut the bottom off of the pineapple and set it aside. Peel the outer layer of the pineapple. Hollow out the inside of your pineapple using a sharp knife and small ice cream scoop. Stuff the pork into your hollowed pineapple. Wrap pineapple with strips of bacon and secure with toothpicks. Sprinkle with Dizzy Pig Pineapple Head Seasoning. Attach the cut bottom to the end of the pineapple with toothpicks. Place grill for one and one half hours or until the internal temperature of the tenderloin reaches 145°F. Slice and enjoy!

Pork T-bone With Walnut Bulgur Pilaf

Servings:4

Cooking Time: 25 Minutes

Ingredients:

- 1 tablespoon unsalted butter
- ½ cup finely chopped yellow onion
- ½ cup chopped California walnuts
- 1 cup bulgur
- 2 tablespoons chopped dried cranberries
- 2 cups chicken stock
- ½ teaspoon salt or salt to taste
- 1 cup apple cider vinegar
- 2 tablespoons molasses
- 2 teaspoons kosher salt or 1 teaspoon plain salt, and additional salt to taste
- 1 teaspoon crushed red pepper flakes
- 2 pork T-bone steaks, or 2 bone-in pork loin chops (about 1¼ lbs. total), about 1 inch thick
- Freshly ground pepper

Directions:

1. Preheat the grill to 350°F using direct heat with a cast iron grate installed.

2. To prepare the pilaf, melt the butter in a dutch oven (or a medium saucepan on the stove top). Add the onion and cook, stirring often, for about 3 minutes. Add the walnuts and stir about 2 minutes more. Add the bulgur and stir to combine. Add the cranberries, stock, and salt (if your stock is salted, you might not need the full amount of salt). Bring to a boil, then cover the pan and cook over low heat for 10–15 minutes, until the bulgur is tender and has absorbed the liquid. The cooked bulgur will stay warm, covered and off heat, for about 20 minutes while you continue with the pork.

3. Season the pork steaks on both sides with salt and ground pepper to taste. Grill on the grill, turning the meat and brushing it with the vinegar baste every 2 minutes. Total cooking time will be 8–10 minutes, until the meat is thoroughly cooked, with no trace of rawness in the center.

4. Serve with the pilaf.

5. To prepare the vinegar baste, in a small sauce pan combine the vinegar, molasses, salt and red pepper flakes. Bring just to a boil, stirring to dissolve the molasses. Set aside.

Grilled Pork Chops With Green Chile-chipotle Relish

Servings:4

Cooking Time: 25 Minutes

Ingredients:

- 1 1⁄2 tbsp seasoned salt
- 1 1⁄2 tbsp coarse-ground black pepper
- 4 (1-inch-thick) bone-in pork chops
- Lime juice
- Meat tenderizer
- Green Chile-Chipotle Relish
- 1 (7-ounce) can chipotle peppers in adobo sauce
- 1 (10-ounce) can Ro*Tel Diced Tomatoes & Green Chiles, drained
- 1 (4-ounce) can green chiles
- 1 cup sugar

Directions:

1. Combine the seasoned salt and pepper in a small bowl. Rub both sides of the pork chops generously with a splash of lime juice. Lightly coat each side of the chops with the meat tenderizer. Repeat with the salt mixture and rub in.

2. Place the chops on a dish, cover, and refrigerate for at least 4 hours, to let the seasonings absorb.

3. Bring the pork chops to room temperature. Preheat the grill to 400°F using direct heat with a cast iron grate installed.

4. Wrap the chops in tin foil and place on the kamado grill for 4-5 minutes per side. Remove the foil from the chops and grill on both sides for 2-3 minutes more, or until medium. Be careful not to overcook because pork easily dries out. Spread with the relish and serve immediately.

5. Remove the chipotle peppers from the can and dice. In a medium saucepan, combine the diced chipotle peppers with adobo sauce, green chiles and sugar. Cook over medium heat for about 10 minutes, stirring frequently, until the sauce thickens slightly and is warmed through. Cool to warm.

6. Tip: Be sure to save any unused relish; it goes great on eggs the next morning or a block of cream cheese for an appetizer!

Korean Pork Riblets

Servings: 6

Cooking Time: 60 Minutes

Ingredients:

- 4 lbs pork riblets
- 3 cups Korean Barbecue Marinade, separated
- 2 cups wood chips, soaked in water for 30 minutes

Directions:

1. Rinse riblets under cold water and pat-dry with a paper towel.
2. Pour 2 cups marinade over pork and let sit for a minimum of 30 minutes.
3. Grilling:
4. Preheat the grill to 225°F using direct heat with a cast iron grate installed.
5. Add wood chips, put the plate setter in place, and place the grid on top.
6. Set the riblets on the grid.
7. Close the dome and allow the ribs to smoke for 30 minutes.
8. Brush the ribs with reserved Korean Barbecue Marinade and close the dome for 30 more minutes, or until the internal temperature reaches 185°F.
9. Once done, remove from the smoker and allow to cool for 15 minutes before carving.
10. Serve with more sauce on the side.

Plts - Pork, Lettuce And Tomato Sandwiches

Servings: 6

Cooking Time: 7 Minutes

Ingredients:

- 6 pork loin chops, cut 1/2 inch thick
- 1/2 tsp garlic powder
- 1/2 tsp onion powder
- 1/2 tsp poultry seasoning
- 1/2 tsp salt
- 1/4 tsp pepper
- 1 cup shredded lettuce
- 1/2 cup mayonnaise
- 2 Tablespoons Besto Pesto
- 12 slices tomato
- 6 sesame seed buns

Directions:

1. Place each pork chop between two pieces of plastic wrap and pound flat.
2. Combine seasonings and sprinkle both sides of each pork chop liberally.
3. Grilling:
4. Preheat the grill to 400°F using direct heat with a cast iron grate installed.
5. Place the chops on the grid and close the dome for 2 minutes.
6. Flip the chops and replace the dome for 3-5 minutes or until the pork is just cooked through.
7. Remove the chops and set aside.
8. Combine mayonnaise and pesto and spread the buns liberally with the mixture.
9. Top each bun with a pork chop, lettuce, and tomato.

Bacon-wrapped Pig Wings

Servings:12

Cooking Time: 90 Minutes

Ingredients:

- 4 one-inch thick boneless pork chops
- 12 slices of bacon (do not used thick sliced)
- Barbecue rub
- Barbecue sauce

Directions:

1. Preheat the grill to 235°F using direct heat with a cast iron grate installed.

2. Cut each pork chop into three strips. To wrap the "wings" start by overlapping the bacon on one end of a pork strip, then wrapping it up and around in a candy-cane fashion. Secure the bacon at the top with a toothpick. Season the bacon-wrapped wings liberally with the rub. Place wings directly on the cooking grid and cook for 90 minutes, or until the bacon is cooked. Serve hot with barbecue sauce for dipping.

Maple-brined, Maple-glazed, Maple-smoked Pork Loin

Servings:6

Cooking Time: 60 Minutes

Ingredients:

- 1 center cut pork loin, whole pork loin or a pork roast can be used
- ¼ cup apple cider vinegar
- 1 cup maple syrup, divided
- ½ cup apple juice
- Favorite BBQ rub
- 1 cup maple syrup, divided
- ½ cup apple cider vinegar
- 1 onion quartered
- ½ cup molasses
- ½ cup brown sugar
- 6 garlic cloves or powder
- 2 tbsp black peppercorns
- ½ cup sea salt or kosher
- 2 bay leaves
- 10 allspice berries
- 8 cups water

Directions:

1. The next day remove the loin from the brine and rinse. Place the loin in cold water 30 minutes prior to cooking.

2. Preheat the grill to 225°F using direct heat with a cast iron grate installed.

3. Mix together the apple cider vinegar, ¼ cup maple syrup, and apple juice. Using an injector, inject the pork 2 times with the mixture. Coat with your favorite BBQ rub.

4. Smoke the pork until the internal temperature reaches 130°F. Glaze with the remaining maple syrup every 30 minutes until the internal temperature reaches 150°F. Remove from the kamado grill and let rest 10 minutes. Slice, serve and enjoy!

5. One day before the cook mix together the brine ingredients and soak the pork loin in the solution overnight.

Caribbean St. Louis Style Ribs

Servings: 6

Cooking Time: 300 Minutes

Ingredients:

- 2 racks (about 4 pounds) St. Louis Style Ribs
- 2 cups Chipotle Mango Lime Sauce
- 1 cup Habanero Rub
- 2 cups wood chips, soaked for 30 minutes in water
- 1/2 cup olive oil
- 1/4 cup lime juice

Directions:

1. Combine olive oil, lime juice, and Habanero Rub. Set aside.
2. Rinse the spare ribs under cold water and pat-dry with a paper towel.
3. Put them on a cutting board, bone side up.
4. Remove the membrane and the flap of meat running along the entire length of the ribs.
5. After trimming, generously apply rub, olive oil, and lime juice mixture.
6. Grilling:
7. Let it sit at room temperature while preheat the grill to 225°F using direct heat with a cast iron grate installed.
8. Add wood chips, put the plate setter in place, and place the grid on top.
9. Set the ribs on the grid, bone side down.
10. Close the dome and allow the ribs to smoke for 3 hours.
11. Brush the ribs with Chipotle Mango Lime Sauce and close the dome for another hour, or until the internal temperature reaches 185°F.
12. Once done, remove from the smoker and allow to cool for 15 minutes before carving.
13. Serve with more sauce on the side.

SIDES

Grilled Polenta

Servings: 8

Cooking Time: 5 Minutes

Ingredients:

- 3 cups water
- 3/4 cups parmesan cheese, grated
- 2 Tablespoons butter
- 1 tsp fresh thyme, chopped
- 1 1/2 cups quick cooking polenta
- 2 tsp salt
- 1 tsp pepper
- Olive oil for brushing

Directions:

1. In a large pot, bring water to a boil with the salt.
2. Slowly whisk in polenta and season with pepper.
3. Continue to whisk until polenta becomes firm.
4. Stir in parmesan and thyme.
5. Pour polenta into a buttered 10 inch springform pan and refrigerate for 1 1/2 - 2 hours or until the polenta is firm.
6. Remove the polenta from the springform pan and slice into 8 pieces.
7. Grilling:
8. Brush both sides with olive oil and place on a 400°F grill.
9. Close the dome and cook for 2 minutes.
10. Turn the polenta, close the dome and continue to cook for another 2 minutes. Serve warm.

Grilled Cabbage With Champagne Vinaigrette

Servings: 6

Cooking Time: 10 Minutes

Ingredients:

- 1 head cabbage
- 2 Tablespoons olive oil
- Salt and Pepper
- 1/2 cup olive oil
- 1/4 cup Champagne vinegar
- 2 Tablespoons capers in brine, drained
- 1 Tablespoon Dijon mustard
- 1 shallot, finely chopped

Directions:

1. Cut the cabbage into 1/2 inch "steaks" from top to root.
2. Brush each side with olive oil and season with salt and pepper.
3. Grilling:
4. Preheat the grill to 425°F using direct heat with a cast iron grate installed and close the lid for 5 minutes.
5. Meanwhile, in a small bowl, combine shallot, mustard, capers, and vinegar.
6. While whisking, stream in olive oil until dressing emulsifies.
7. Flip cabbage steaks and cook on the other side for an additional 5 minutes with the dome closed.
8. Remove cabbage from the grill to a platter and pour dressing over top. Serve warm.

Creamed Corn

Servings: 6

Cooking Time: 30 Minutes

Ingredients:

- 1 cup heavy cream
- 1/4 cup parmesan cheese
- 2 (10 oz) packages of frozen sweet corn
- 1 lime, zested and juiced
- 1 tsp sriracha
- 1 tsp salt
- 1/2 tsp pepper

Directions:

1. Combine all ingredients, minus the lime juice in the dutch oven.
2. Grilling:
3. Preheat the grill to 350°F using direct heat with a cast iron grate installed.
4. Cover and close the dome for 30 minutes.
5. Add lime juice and serve.

Wood-plank Loaded Mashed Potatoes

Servings: 16

Cooking Time: 50 Minutes

Ingredients:

- 1lb (450g) red potatoes
- 1lb (450g) Yukon Gold potatoes
- 1 tbsp kosher salt, plus 1 tsp
- 2 strips bacon, diced
- 2 tbsp unsalted butter
- 1⁄4 cup sour cream
- 1⁄4 cup heavy cream
- 4oz (113g) shredded Cheddar cheese, plus more for topping
- 4 scallions, thinly sliced, plus more for topping
- freshly ground black pepper

Directions:

1. Place a 4 x 9in (10 x 23cm) cedar wood plank in a baking dish, cover with cold water, and place heavy cans or stones on the plank to keep it submerged. Soak for 1 to 2 hours.

2. Place red potatoes and Yukon Gold potatoes in a large stockpot and add cold water to cover by several inches. Place the pot on the stovetop over high heat, add 1 tsp salt, and bring to a boil. Reduce to a simmer, cover, and cook until potatoes are fork tender, about 25 minutes. Drain potatoes, reserving 1 cup cooking water.

3. Preheat the grill to 350°F (177°C) using direct heat with a standard grate installed and a cast iron skillet on the grate. Add bacon to the hot skillet, and cook until bacon is crisp and the fat has rendered, about 10 to 15 minutes, stirring occasionally. Transfer the cooked bacon pieces to a plate lined with a paper towel.

4. In a large bowl, combine potatoes, butter, sour cream, heavy cream, Cheddar cheese, scallions, bacon, and 1 tbsp salt. Mash with a potato masher until potatoes have broken down and cheese and sour cream are fully incorporated. If potatoes are too stiff, add some of the reserved cooking water.

5. Place the soaked plank on the grate and allow it to heat for 2 to 5 minutes, then flip it over. Scoop the mashed potatoes onto the heated side of the plank. Top the potatoes with a little Cheddar cheese, close the lid, and cook until cheese has melted and potatoes have browned slightly, about 7 to 10 minutes. Remove potatoes from the grill, sprinkle with scallions, and serve immediately.

Grilled Lemon Garlic Zucchini

Servings: 6

Cooking Time: 5 Minutes

Ingredients:

- 4 zucchini, sliced lengthwise into 1/2 inch slices
- 1/4 cup butter, softened
- 2 tsp parsley, chopped
- 3 cloves garlic, minced
- The zest and juice of 1 lemon

Directions:

1. In a small dish, combine butter, parsley, garlic, lemon zest, and lemon juice.
2. Liberally brush each zucchini slice with the butter mixture.
3. Grilling:
4. Place the zucchini on a 500°F grill and close the dome for 3 minutes.
5. Flip the zucchini and recover with the dome for an additional 2 minutes.
6. Drizzle remaining butter on top of zucchini as it comes off the grill. Serve warm.

Grilled Endive Salad

Servings: 6

Cooking Time: 2 Minutes

Ingredients:

- 2 cups frisee
- 1/2 cup pecan halves
- 1/4 cup dried cranberries
- 1/4 cup crumbled bacon
- 2 heads endive
- 1 bunch spinach, cleaned and stems removed
- 1/4 cup olive oil
- 2 Tablespoons Dijon Mustard
- 1 Tablespoon honey
- 1 shallot, finely minced
- The juice of 1 lemon
- Kosher salt and fresh cracked pepper to taste

Directions:

1. In a large bowl, combine dressing ingredients. Set aside.
2. Grilling:
3. Split endive down the middle, lengthwise and preheat the grill to 425°F using direct heat with a cast iron grate installed.
4. Remove the endive and slice into half rounds.
5. Toss shredded frisee, sliced endive, spinach, pecans, and cranberries in the dressing and serve immediately.

Asiago & Sage Scalloped Potatoes

Servings: 10

Cooking Time: 60 Minutes

Ingredients:

- 2 tbsp unsalted butter
- 2 medium yellow onions, thinly sliced
- 1/2 tsp finely chopped garlic
- 2 bay leaves
- 1/4 tsp grated fresh nutmeg
- 1 tbsp kosher salt
- 3/4 tsp ground black pepper
- 11/4 cups heavy cream
- 1/2 cup whole milk
- 2 tbsp finely chopped fresh sage
- 21/2lb (1.1kg) Idaho potatoes, peeled and thinly sliced
- for the topping
- 1 cup freshly grated Asiago cheese, about 3oz (85g) in total
- 1 cup plain breadcrumbs
- 2 tbsp extra virgin olive oil
- 1/4 tsp kosher salt
- 1/4 tsp ground black pepper
- 11/2 tsp finely chopped fresh sage

Directions:

1. Preheat the grill to 400°F (204°C) using indirect heat with a standard grate installed. Place a large heavy-bottomed saucepan on the grate and melt butter. Add onions, close the lid, and grill until golden brown, about 8 minutes, stirring often.

2. Add garlic, bay leaves, nutmeg, salt, and pepper, and cook for 30 seconds. Add heavy cream and milk, and bring to a boil. Remove from the heat, cover, and let sit for 5 minutes. Remove bay leaves and stir in sage.

3. To make the topping, in a medium bowl, toss cheese with breadcrumbs, olive oil, salt, pepper, and sage.

4. In a large bowl, gently toss potatoes with the onion mixture. Spread half the potatoes and liquid in a 2-quart (2-liter) grill-safe baking dish and sprinkle 2/3 cup of the cheese and breadcrumb mixture over top. Add the remaining potatoes to the dish, pressing firmly to pack them down. Spoon any remaining liquid over the potatoes and cover with the remaining breadcrumbs.

5. Place the dish on the grate, close the grill lid, and cook until potatoes are fork tender and the top is golden brown, about 1 hour. (If the top browns too quickly, loosely cover the dish with aluminum foil). Remove potatoes from the grill and serve hot.

Grilled Paneer

Servings: 6

Cooking Time: 30 Minutes

Ingredients:

- 4 tbsp unsalted butter
- 1 medium white onion, diced
- 3 tbsp chopped fresh ginger
- 1 jalapeño pepper, diced
- 1 tbsp vindaloo curry powder
- 1 tsp kosher salt, divided
- 28oz (800g) can whole peeled tomatoes, preferably fire roasted
- 1/2 tsp ground cinnamon
- 2 tbsp crushed lime leaves
- 3 tbsp honey
- 1/2 cup heavy cream
- 1lb (450g) paneer cheese, thickly sliced
- 8oz (225g) arugula
- 1/4 cup chopped fresh cilantro
- naan bread, to serve (optional)

Directions:

1. Preheat the grill to 425°F (218°C) using direct heat with a cast iron grate installed and cast iron skillet or an all-metal saucepan on the grate. Once hot, add butter to the skillet, stirring until melted, then stir in onion, ginger, and jalapeño. Sprinkle curry powder and 1/2 tsp salt over top and cook until onions begin to soften and brown, about 5 to 7 minutes, stirring occasionally.

2. Add tomatoes, cinnamon, lime leaves, and honey, pressing tomatoes with a wooden spoon to break them down. Cook uncovered until the sauce thickens and only a little liquid remains, about10 to 15 minutes, stirring occasionally.

3. Transfer the sauce to a blender (or use an immersion blender), and purée on high speed a until smooth, about 1 minute. Wipe the skillet clean and return to the grill. Pour the sauce through a fine mesh strainer back into the skillet. Stir in cream and the remaining 1/2 tsp salt, adding more of each to taste.

4. Place paneer on the grate, close the lid, and cook until the cheese has visible grill marks, about 2 to 3 minutes per side. Cut into large cubes and add to the curry sauce. Gently stir in arugula and half the cilantro. Sprinkle the remaining cilantro over top, and serve immediately with warmed naan (if desired).

Corn & Tomato Salsa

Servings: 8
Cooking Time: 10 Minutes

Ingredients:

- 6 ears of corn, shucked
- 1 lime, halved
- 1 avocado, halved
- 1lb (450g) grape tomatoes, quartered
- 1/2 tsp kosher salt, plus more as needed
- 1/2 tsp ground black pepper, plus more as needed
- 2 tsp olive oil
- 4oz (110g) blue cheese, crumbled
- 10 fresh basil leaves, sliced

Directions:

1. Preheat the grill to 425°F (218°C) using direct heat with a cast iron grate installed. Place corn, avocado, and lime on the grate, close the lid, and grill until beginning to soften and char, about 7 to 10 minutes. Transfer the corn, avocado, and lime to a cutting board. Cut the kernels from the corn and dice the avocado.

2. In a large bowl, gently combine corn, tomatoes, avocado, salt, and pepper. Squeeze the grilled lime over top, drizzle with olive oil, and toss to coat.

3. Top the corn mixture with blue cheese and basil, and toss one final time. Season with salt and pepper to taste. Serve immediately.

Thanksgiving Stuffing

Servings: 8
Cooking Time: 45 Minutes

Ingredients:

- 8 ounces bulk breakfast sausage
- 4 cups cornbread, crumbled
- 4 cups sourdough bread, cut in cubes
- 1/2 cup onion, diced
- 1/2 cup celery, diced
- 1/2 cup Granny Smith apple, diced
- 4 Tablespoons butter, softened
- 2 cups chicken broth
- 1 tsp poultry seasoning

Directions:

1. Preheat the grill to 375°F using direct heat with a cast iron grate installed with the dutch oven on the grid.
2. Cook breakfast sausage in the dutch oven until brown.
3. Add onion and celery and cook until soft, about 5 minutes.
4. Add apple and cook an additional 2 minutes.
5. Stir in crumbled cornbread and sourdough bread cubes.
6. Pour chicken broth over mixture and season with poultry seasoning.
7. Dot the top of the stuffing with butter, cover, and lower the dome.
8. Cook the stuffing for 30 minutes. Serve warm.

German Potato Salad

Servings: 8
Cooking Time: 70 Minutes

Ingredients:

- 2lb (1kg) Yukon Gold potatoes, unpeeled and cut into rounds or bite-sized pieces
- 1/2lb (225g) thick-cut bacon
- 3/4 cup finely chopped yellow onion
- 1/3 cup white vinegar
- 1/4 cup sugar
- 1 tbsp Dijon mustard
- 1 tsp kosher salt
- 2 tbsp minced chives, to garnish

Directions:

1. Preheat the grill to 350ºF (177°C) using indirect heat with a cast iron grate installed and a cast iron skillet on the grate. Place potatoes on the grate around the skillet, close the lid, and roast until fork tender, about 45 minutes. Remove potatoes from the grill and set aside.
2. Add bacon to the hot skillet, close the lid, and cook until crisp, about 10 to 15 minutes. Once crisp, transfer to a plate lined with a paper towel and crumble into small pieces. Pour off the rendered fat, reserving 4 tbsp in the skillet.
3. Add onion to the skillet, close the lid, and cook until translucent and beginning to brown, about 4 to 5 minutes. Whisk in vinegar, sugar, mustard, and salt, and stir until thick and bubbly, about 2 to 3 minutes. Add the cooked potatoes, and toss to coat.
4. Remove the skillet from the grill, top with crumbled bacon, and garnish with chives. Serve warm.

Breakfast Casserole

Servings: 6
Cooking Time: 40 Minutes

Ingredients:

- 1 lb bulk pork breakfast sausage
- 1 (16 oz) bag of frozen O'Brien style hash browns
- 1 dozen eggs, beaten
- 1/4 cup grated onion
- 1/4 tsp black pepper
- Hot sauce for garnish

Directions:

1. Preheat the grill to 350°F using direct heat with a cast iron grate installed with the dutch oven on the grid.
2. Brown sausage with onion in the dutch oven.
3. Add hash browns and stir to combine.
4. Add eggs and cover.
5. Lower the dome for 15 minutes or until the eggs are just cooked through.
6. Serve the casserole with hot sauce for garnish.

Cowboy Caviar

Servings: 8
Cooking Time: 10 Minutes

Ingredients:

- 2 ears fresh corn on the cob
- 1 large tomato, finely diced
- 1 bell pepper, finely diced
- 1 jalapeño, very finely chopped
- 1/4 cup bottled Italian salad dressing
- 2 cans black beans, drained and rinsed
- 1 can pinto beans, drained and rinsed

Directions:

1. Place shucked and cleaned ears of corn on a 425°F grill and close the dome for 5 minutes.
2. Turn the corn and close the dome for another 5 minutes before removing and setting aside.
3. Assembly:
4. Carefully cut the corn off the cob and place it in a large bow.
5. Add remaining ingredients and toss to combine.

Mexican Street Corn

Servings: 6
Cooking Time: 10 Minutes

Ingredients:

- 6 ears corn
- 1/2 cup cotija cheese
- 1 Tablespoon chili powder
- 1 cup mayonnaise
- 1 lime, cut into wedges

Directions:

1. Pull back the husk of the corn and thoroughly remove the silk from each ear of corn.
2. Soak the corn in water for 20 minutes before cooking.
3. Peel back the husks to reveal the corn.
4. Grilling:
5. Preheat the grill to 450°F using direct heat with a cast iron grate installed.
6. Close the dome for 5 minutes, turn the corn, and close the dome for an additional 5 minutes.
7. Remove the corn from the grill. Spread with mayonnaise, sprinkle with chili powder, and coat with cotija cheese.
8. Serve with lime wedges.

Corn & Poblano Pudding

Servings: 8
Cooking Time: 30 Minutes

Ingredients:

- vegetable oil, for greasing
- 4 ears of sweet corn, shucked
- 1 poblano pepper, left whole
- 4 large eggs
- 1 cup whole milk
- 1/2 tsp kosher salt
- 1/4 tsp ground nutmeg
- 1/4 tsp ground cayenne pepper
- 2oz (55g) shredded Cheddar cheese

Directions:

1. Preheat the grill to 350°F (177°C) using indirect heat with a standard grate installed. Grease a cast iron skillet with oil.

2. Place corn and pepper on the grate, positioning them around the edges, close the lid, and grill until beginning to soften and char, about 10 minutes. Transfer the vegetables to a cutting board, cut the kernels from the cobs, and seed and dice the pepper.

3. In a large bowl, whisk together eggs, milk, salt, nutmeg, cayenne, and cheese until well combined. Stir in corn kernels and pepper. Pour the mixture into the greased dish and place on the grate. Close the lid and bake until a knife inserted halfway between the center and the outer edge comes out clean, about 20 minutes. Remove the pudding from the grill and serve warm or at room temperature.

Prosciutto And Pear Bruschetta

Servings: 6
Cooking Time: 5 Minutes

Ingredients:

- 4 oz prosciutto
- 4 oz shaved parmesan cheese
- 1 cup baby arugula
- 1 baguette, sliced 1/2 inch thick
- 1 pear, sliced thin
- 2 Tablespoons olive oil
- 2 Tablespoons high quality balsamic vinegar

Directions:

1. Brush each baguette slice with olive oil and place on a 325°F grill with the dome closed for 5 minutes.
2. Assembly:
3. Remove bread slices and top each with prosciutto, pear slices, parmesan, and baby arugula.
4. Drizzle a few drops of balsamic vinegar over each bruschetta and serve.

Cheesy Tomato Risotto

Servings: 6
Cooking Time: 35 Minutes

Ingredients:

- 1 tbsp unsalted butter
- 1⁄2 red onion, chopped
- 3 garlic cloves, minced
- 3⁄4 cup Arborio rice
- 3 cups chicken stock, warmed, plus more as needed
- 2 medium Roma tomatoes, diced small
- 2oz (55g) freshly shredded Parmesan cheese
- 2 scallions, thinly sliced
- 1 tbsp chopped fresh flat-leaf parsley

Directions:

1. Preheat the grill to 350ºF (177°C) using indirect heat with a standard grate installed and a dutch oven on the grate. In the hot dutch oven, melt butter. Add onion and garlic, close the grill lid, and cook until barely beginning to soften, about 2 minutes. Add rice, stir, and close the grill lid. Cook until rice is coated with butter and slightly toasted, about 2 to 3 minutes.
2. Add warm stock to the rice 1 cup at a time, stirring often. Add more stock only after the liquid from the previous addition is absorbed. (This will take about 10 minutes each time you add the liquid.) Add tomatoes and cheese, and stir until cheese melts. Add scallions and parsley, and stir until just combined. Remove the dutch oven from the grill and serve immediately.

Grilled Artichokes

Servings: 4
Cooking Time: 7 Minutes

Ingredients:

- 4 large artichokes
- 2 Tablespoons olive oil
- 1 lemon
- Salt and pepper
- 1/2 cup mayonnaise
- 2 Tablespoons lemon juice
- 2 Tablespoons basil pesto
- 1/2 tsp sriracha

Directions:

1. Trim artichokes of their fibrous ends and thorny leaves.
2. Quarter the artichokes and remove the thistle in the middle.
3. Rub all cut ends with half of a lemon to prevent browning.
4. In a large steamer, cook artichokes 45 minutes or until just fork tender.
5. Brush each artichoke with olive oil and season with salt and pepper.
6. Grilling:
7. Preheat the grill to 425°F using direct heat with a cast iron grate installed and close the dome for 3 minutes.
8. Turn the artichokes and close the dome for another 2-4 minutes.
9. Serve with dipping sauce.

Smoked Potato Salad

Servings: 8

Cooking Time: 120 Minutes

Ingredients:

- 4 large baking potatoes
- 4 large eggs, hard boiled and finely chopped
- 2 green onions, finely chopped
- 2 large dill pickles, finely chopped
- 1 rib celery, finely diced
- 1/2 cup mayonnaise
- The juice of 1 lemon
- 1/2 tsp black pepper
- 1/2 tsp celery seed
- 1/2 tsp dried dill

Directions:

1. Scrub the potatoes.
2. Grilling:
3. Place the potatoes alongside meat that is smoking at 225°F.
4. Assembly:
5. When the potatoes are fork tender, chill in the refrigerator for 30 minutes.
6. Peel and cut potatoes into small cubes.
7. In a large bowl, combine dressing ingredients.
8. Add potatoes, eggs, green onion, pickle, and celery to the dressing and gently toss

Parmesan Zucchini Spears

Servings: 4

Cooking Time: 10 Minutes

Ingredients:

- 4 zucchini, cut in half, then cut into quarters lengthwise
- 1/2 cup parmesan, grated
- 1 tsp Italian seasoning
- 1/2 tsp garlic powder
- Salt and Pepper to taste
- Olive oil for brushing

Directions:

1. Brush each zucchini spear with olive oil and season with salt and pepper.
2. In a small bowl, combine Italian seasoning, garlic powder, and parmesan.
3. Place zucchini spears on a small sheet tray and sprinkle the parmesan over each spear.
4. Grilling:
5. Place the sheet tray on the grid of a 500°F grill.
6. Close the dome and cook for 10 minutes or until the parmesan is golden brown. Serve warm.

Alligator Eggs

Servings: 6

Cooking Time: 10 Minutes

Ingredients:

- 8 ounces cream cheese, softened
- 1 cup sharp cheddar cheese
- 12 thin slices bacon
- 6 jalapeños

Directions:

1. Slice jalapeños in half and remove seeds. Set aside.
2. In a small bowl, combine cheddar cheese and cream cheese until mixed.
3. Stuff 2 Tablespoon of the cream cheese mixture into each jalapeño half.
4. Wrap each jalapeño half in one strip of bacon, securing with a toothpick.
5. Grilling:
6. Preheat the grill to 425°F using direct heat with a cast iron grate installed.
7. Place the alligator eggs directly on the grid and close the dome for 10 minutes or until the bacon is crisp. Serve immediately.

www.ingramcontent.com/pod-product-compliance
Lightning Source LLC
Chambersburg PA
CBHW080453030726
47592CB00011B/3094

CHAR-GRILLER

CERAMIC CHARCOAL

GRILL COOKBOOK 2000

2000 DAYS EASY AND DELICIOUS RECIPES TO ENJOY WITH YOUR FAMILY, WITH THE BEST TECHNIQUES USED BY MASTERS

ANGELICA TURNER

Copyright © 2021 by Angelica Turner - All rights reserved.

The content contained within this book may not be reproduced, duplicated, or transmitted without direct written permission from the author or the publisher. Under no circumstances will any blame or legal responsibility be held against the publisher, or author, for any damages, reparation, or monetary loss due to the information contained within this book, either directly or indirectly.

Legal Notice: This book is copyright protected. It is only for personal use. You cannot amend, distribute, sell, use, quote or paraphrase any part, or the content within this book, without the consent of the author or publisher.

Disclaimer Notice: Please note the information contained within this document is for educational and entertainment purposes only. All effort has been executed to present accurate, up to date, reliable, complete information. No warranties of any kind are declared or implied. Readers acknowledge that the author is not engaged in the rendering of legal, financial, medical, or professional advice. The content within this book has been derived from various sources. Please consult a licensed professional before attempting any techniques outlined in this book. By reading this document, the reader agrees that under no circumstances is the author responsible for any losses, direct or indirect, that are incurred as a result of the use of the information contained within this document, including, but not limited to, errors, omissions, or inaccuracies.